D1129827

CELEBRATE

PLANT-BASED RECIPES FOR EVERY OCCASION

Bettina Campolucci-Bordi

Photography by
Louise Hagger

Hardie Grant

BOOKS

CONTENTS

ABOUT THIS BOOK

Our English word celebrate comes from the Latin *celebrare*, meaning 'to assemble to honour'. To celebrate means to mark a special day, event or holiday. You might celebrate a birthday, a holiday, a religious event like Easter, an occasion or an anniversary.

To me, this book is a celebration of food, community, cooking and being together with the people we love. The idea of this book was born over a year ago when the world was a different place. The irony is that I wrote the book during 2020, the year we had to figure out other ways to celebrate than being together with our nearest and dearest.

I hope from here on in we can make up for that time and celebrate as much as we possibly can! Dinner parties, birthdays, anniversaries, Christmas, Easter, barbecues and more. Let's celebrate the little things, the big things and be together.

The recipes in this book are grouped according to different occasions. All are plant-based, and I try to use local and seasonal ingredients where possible. I am also aware that practicality and ease play a role too and that not everyone has the same opportunity to source particular ingredients, as this depends on how accessible they are and where in the world you live and the climate. I wanted the ingredients to be accessible and affordable while also enabling you to include plants in ways that are easy, tasty and planet-friendly. With all that in mind, I hope there are options for everyone, from turning a bag of frozen peas into the most delicious fritters to finding uses for the humble swede (rutabaga) that appears in our vegetable boxes. I hope you all find your favourite recipes and use them to celebrate with your loved ones.

Here's to health, happiness and love.
Lots of love and celebrations,

Bettina xxx

ABOUT THE AUTHOR

Hi Lovely,

Bettina here. I am a self-taught chef and a hugely passionate advocate for plants. I specialise in plant-based (vegan) and free-from recipe development for brands and the hospitality industry and also within food advancement. I have written two cookbooks, *Happy Food* and *7 Day Vegan Challenge*, and this is my third. I work freelance and run Health & Wellness Retreats as a Retreat Chef. I also run my Retreat Chef Academy where I teach all these food concepts along with sustainability and waste-free principles, which, as a Retreat Chef, you adopt right from the get-go. I am passionate about unravelling the potential of plant foods and the free-from area by establishing easy and basic principles that incorporate seasonality and local produce – food that makes you feel good, is grown within the seasons, and nurtured by people who care.

From the very beginning

To really understand my background and where my love of food began, let's go back to the beginning. My father is Norwegian, my mother Bulgarian/Danish, and me? Well, I was born in Denmark, but lived for the first 11 years of my life in East Africa, Tanzania to be precise, and after that in Sweden. In Tanzania, I used to go with my mother to the food markets to pick our fruits and vegetables, and I quickly learned the art of haggling for the best quality and price. We also used to visit a small farmer with just a few cows. I would sit in the back of the car with a bucketful of fresh milk that my mother would magically turn into butter, cream and yoghurt. I learned early on that good things were worth waiting for. There is a running joke about my father taking his time to cook because by the time the food was ready, we would all be starving! He would spend hours getting all the ingredients ready, meticulously organised in between sips of wine and chatting – making sure each element of the dish was cooked properly and was just right.

Our holidays were spent in Bulgaria with my grandmother and auntie, who were both amazing cooks. I used to sit at the kitchen table at my auntie's house watching her make pineapple upside-down cake, crème brûlée, stews and breads baked from scratch – all on their way to the feasts that would be conjured up on our arrival. Other summers were spent on the other side of the globe in Scandinavia, Sweden, where my other grandmother lived. Again, an amazing cook with green fingers who has all sorts of wonders growing in her garden and a tiny summerhouse in the woods. Jams, cordials and pickling were her speciality.

I come from the sort of family that does not remember visits to museums or art galleries – instead, my holiday memories are filled with dishes, markets and food experiences. We travelled extensively as a family, gathering food memories, and that has stayed with me to this day. I love travelling, sampling and experiencing different cultures and countries through food. There are untold stories everywhere and these are such a huge part of our lives. It's magic, really – and that's how I initially caught the food bug, which has blossomed into a life-encompassing passion that won't be going anywhere soon.

The beginning of Bettina's Kitchen

My original background is in the hotel industry. I have a BBA in Hotel Management & Business and studied in Switzerland, Ireland and Spain. However, I was always front of house. That background helped immensely when I got into the wellness industry in 2011, running health retreats in Spain and later all over the world.

Cooking has been a constant in my life. I have loved it right from the start and remember my first dish being pancakes when I was six years old. It is my daughter's too now and a family staple at the weekends. Despite my passion for cooking, it did not become my career until my late 20s, so remember: it's never too late to start working with your passion.

For me, cooking became a way of inspiring people to include and cook with ingredients that can sometimes seem daunting. I wanted to show others how food could be inspiring and where it comes from, and that cooking from scratch is the single most powerful thing you can do for yourself and your family. The retreats were the initial stage in spreading this message.

My lifelong passion for food meant I appointed myself retreat cook and my hobby quickly transformed into my career as a chef specialising in plant-based cuisine. From here, I specialised in gluten-free and free-from recipes, which form the foundations of my cooking.

I went on to study at the Matthew Kenney Culinary Academy, in Los Angeles, to expand my cooking skills and knowledge and to learn the culinary arts. I also enjoyed extensive travelling and discovering how other cultures cook and use plant foods. I started sharing recipes on Instagram and slowly but surely people wanted more, and Bettina's Kitchen was born.

Fast forward a few years and books. I am now living in the United Kingdom and my passion is still very much plant-based cuisine. However, I am keen to include as much local and seasonal produce as possible, and I am always focusing on making the vegetable the hero ingredient on our plates.

Bettina's Kitchen today encompasses culinary, yoga and mindfulness retreats, plant-based cooking workshops, recipe development, food writing, the Retreat Chef Academy and my cookbooks. Everything I do honours my own beliefs about food and wellness and aligns with my philosophies: that we should eat seasonally, locally and from farm to table as much as possible; we should support small businesses within our communities; we must use roots, shoots and all! Cooking waste-free is particularly important to me and we should also let our veggies do the talking – the best plant food is fuss-free, simple, easy, inexpensive and speaks for itself.

The last few years have been quite an adventure. Combining healthy cooking with travel and wellness worldwide, you can find me cooking on and training local kitchen teams through my newest venture, The Retreat Agency, with my co-founder Jools. My favourite retreat work includes introducing people to remote, magical places, including Mongolia, Panama and Ecuador. I also host my very own retreat once or twice a year in my favourite place in the world, Bali. The rest of the year you can cook with me and learn from my experience by joining one of the Retreat Chef Academies that I run a few times a year. It is a one-week intensive course where I teach you everything that I have learned over my years in the wellness industry.

My knowledge of, and passion for, plant-based foods continue to grow, and I am constantly on the hunt for delicious solutions to the belief that eating plants is boring, expensive and time-consuming. I hope that I can help to inspire you to incorporate more plants in your diet, provide a starting point for your journey, and show you just how easy cooking with plants can be. I believe we can now start to positively influence the next generation in the importance of true self-care and choices, so that, unlike us, they don't have to relearn them later in life. This includes sourcing local ingredients in any shape or form, preserving traditions, respecting the seasons and cooking from scratch. Last but not least: celebrate food, life, friendships and all the good in the world.

NOTES ON THE RECIPES

MAKE-AHEAD, FREEZABLE AND GLUTEN-FREE

All the recipes in the book are marked with these brilliant little symbols. Many of them can be made ahead of time and put together just as your guests are arriving, to keep things fresh and give you enough time to mingle and avoid being stuck in the kitchen. Some of the recipes can also be prepared in advance and frozen to save time and stress during big occasions, Christmas being one of those. I have also consciously marked the gluten-free recipes. I know my previous books were completely gluten-free, but I really wanted to make this book more accessible. There are still some great gluten-free recipes in here (clearly marked) and even baking options at the back.

A NOTE ON INGREDIENTS

I am a firm believer in following the seasons: produce tastes better, is often better priced and you get to support local farms and businesses. If you don't have the time to go to farmers' markets, then subscribing to a local veggie box can be a great option. Trial your way through a few boxes until you find the perfect fit.

You might not get it all right immediately – finding good produce or a service that fits your lifestyle can take time and effort – but, trust me, it'll be worth it in the end.

WASTE NOT

I have made a conscious decision to use the same ingredients in many of the recipes, so that you won't need a pantry filled with fancy items to be able to cook from the book. Also, you will be able to minimise waste, as a couple of pounds of carrots, for example, will lend themselves well to several of the recipes. I also love using roots, shoots, tops and all of the veggies – leek tops, cauliflower leaves, the lot! I have made sure that the recipes are simple and easy to follow, so you don't spend too much time planning or preparing meals.

A LITTLE NOTE ON EQUIPMENT

You don't need any special equipment for the simple and recognisable cooking methods used in this book. I do use a food blender or processor a lot, so that's the only essential, but even a handheld blender with the right attachment will do fine. And, in order to do my bit for the environment, I prefer to use glass containers and bottles for buying and storing food instead of plastic.

DINNER AT MINE

This chapter is filled with the food I love to eat and prepare for my friends and loved ones: feasting platters, little bowls of dips and sauces, slaws and all. I adore the concept of having a little bit of everything on my plate. Discovering flavour combinations that work really well and using your senses to pick out your favourite bits. This is communal food at its best, encompassing all my preferred elements.

CRUSHED CRISPED NEW POTATOES
WITH SOUR CREAM & DILL
—PAGE 16—

GREEN CORN FRITTERS
WITH RAITA & CHUTNEY
—PAGE 17—

HERBED CROSTINIS
WITH LEEK & TAHINI DIP
—PAGE 18—

CRUSHED CRISPED NEW POTATOES WITH SOUR CREAM & DILL

I am a huge potato fan, and these little nuggets of goodness are one of my favourite ways of eating them. So crispy and dolloped with a salty fresh sour cream and dill and chive topping, this is a marriage made in heaven.

SERVES
4–6

INGREDIENTS

1 kg (2 lb 4 oz) new potatoes
olive oil, for basting
salt and pepper

FOR THE TOPPING:

200 g (7 oz/scant 1 cup) plant
    yoghurt or sour cream
20 g (¾ oz) dill fronds
1 tablespoon chopped chives
2 tablespoons chopped cornichons
juice of ½ a lemon
1 teaspoon Dijon mustard
1 tablespoon chopped red
   or green chillies
salt and pepper

TO SERVE:

2 spring onions (scallions),
   finely sliced
handful of dill fronds

METHOD

Preheat the oven to 180°C (350°F/gas 4).

Cook the new potatoes in a large saucepan of boiling water for 15–20 minutes, until soft, then drain well and allow to cool a little.

Line a large baking tray (pan) with baking parchment and drizzle with a thin layer of olive oil. Add the cooked potatoes and use the palm of your hand to cover and gently smash each one down, so they stay intact but split slightly – they should be pretty flat so the surface will crisp up really nicely.

Baste the potatoes with 2–3 tablespoons of olive oil and a generous sprinkling of salt and pepper. Roast in the oven for 20–30 minutes, or until nice and crispy.

While the potatoes are roasting, mix all the ingredients for the topping in a bowl and and set aside.

Once the potatoes are ready, remove from the oven and arrange on a serving platter. Add dollops of topping over the potatoes and sprinkle with the spring onions and dill fronds. These potatoes are fantastic served as canapés or as part of a pick-n-mix dinner.

GREEN CORN FRITTERS WITH RAITA & CHUTNEY

The great thing about these fritters is that they look intricate but are so easy to make and put together. Best of all, they pack a slight punch!

MAKES 20

METHOD

Add all the ingredients for the fritters (aside from the reserved corn) to a food processor or blender and blitz to form a batter (it's fine to use the corn from frozen).

To make the raita, mix all the ingredients together in a bowl and keep in the fridge.

Heat a layer of oil in a large frying pan (skillet). Using an ice-cream scoop (if you have one) pour out small fritters from the mixture and fry for a few minutes on each side until crisp and golden.

Just before your guests arrive, put a layer of chutney on each fritter, then a dollop of raita, and finish with a topping of chives, coriander and pomegranate seeds. Serve the fritters on a beautiful tray.

COOK'S TIP:

The fritters can be made earlier and kept at an ambient room temperature, covered with a dish towel to keep them moist.

INGREDIENTS

FOR THE FRITTERS:

180 g (6¼ oz) sweetcorn
    (frozen or fresh), saving 50 g
    (2 oz) of kernels to mix in whole
45 g (1¾ oz) spinach leaves
75 g (2½ oz/¾ cup) chickpea
    (gram) flour
⅛ teaspoon bicarbonate
    of soda (baking soda)
½ teaspoon baking powder
1 tablespoon curry powder
180 ml (6 fl oz/¾ cup) plant milk
    (I like oat milk)
salt and pepper, to taste
oil, for frying

FOR THE RAITA:

200 g (7 oz/scant 1 cup)
    plant yoghurt
1 carrot, grated
1 cucumber, deseeded and
    finely chopped
¼ red onion, finely chopped
10 g (½ oz) mint leaves,
    finely chopped
juice of 1 lemon

TOPPINGS:

chutney (either storebought
    or homemade)
handful of snipped chives
handful of coriander
    (cilantro) leaves
handful of pomegranate seeds

HERBED CROSTINIS
WITH LEEK & TAHINI DIP

/

Have you ever wondered what to do with
your leeks? Let me introduce you to the
sweetest, creamiest dip ever. I use stalks
and all when I cook down leeks and slow
cooking them introduces a sweetness that
is hard to beat. This will become your
staple, I promise.

⟳
_____

SERVES
4–6

INGREDIENTS

1 baguette, sliced into rounds,
    or 4–6 slices of sourdough,
    cut in half

FOR THE LEEK AND TAHINI DIP:

3 leeks
3–4 tablespoons olive oil
4 dates, pitted and torn
3–4 tablespoons tahini
2 teaspoons ground sumac
juice of 1 lemon
salt and pepper

FOR THE GREEN OIL:

30 g (1 oz) flat-leaf parsley, chopped
2 garlic cloves, grated
3 tablespoons olive oil

TO SERVE:

baby gem lettuce leaves (optional)
handful of pine nuts
olive oil, to drizzle

○
METHOD

Preheat the oven to 180°C (350°F/gas 4).

Cut the leeks in half lengthwise, then place in basin of
warm water and wash between the layers until fully clean.

Thinly slice the leeks, green parts and all, and add to
a large saucepan with the olive oil and a generous pinch
of salt. Fry the leeks over a high heat for 5 minutes, then
turn down to a medium heat for a further 15–20 minutes.

While the leeks are cooking, put all the ingredients for the
green oil in a food processor or blender and whizz until
combined. You can also use a hand-held blender for this.

Take the sliced baguette/sourdough, spread some green
oil on each piece and place on a baking tray (pan).

When the leeks are ready, add to a food processor or blender,
along with the dates, tahini, sumac and lemon juice, and
pulse to make a chunky dip.

Bake the herbed garlic bread in the oven for 5–10 minutes,
or until nicely crisped.

Arrange the bread around the outside of a nice platter and
place the dip in the middle. You can also add some baby
gem lettuce as a dipping option alongside the bread.

Top the leek dip with some pine nuts and a drizzle of
olive oil.

PEA & MINT FRITTERS WITH GARLIC MAYO

SERVES
4–6

If you happen to have a bag of frozen peas lying around in your freezer, then I urge you to make these epic fritters. They are so simple, but I think one of my best little inventions. Dipped in a quick garlic mayo, what's not to like?

INGREDIENTS

FOR THE FRITTERS:

250 g (9 oz) potatoes, peeled
1 red onion, sliced into half-moons
olive oil, for frying
500 g (1 lb 2 oz) frozen peas
35 g (1¼ oz/⅓ cup) chickpea
    (gram) flour
handful of mint leaves, chopped
salt and pepper, to taste
lemon wedges, to serve

FOR THE GARLIC MAYO:

200 g (7 oz/¾ cup) plant mayonnaise
30 g (1 oz) chives, snipped
½ garlic clove, peeled and grated
juice of ½ lemon
salt and pepper, to taste

METHOD

Cook the potatoes in a saucepan of boiling water, drain well, then mash in a big bowl.

Fry the onion in some olive oil in a saucepan over a medium heat for 5–10 minutes until caramelised. Set aside.

Add the peas to a food processor or blender and pulse until almost smooth, but still slightly chunky. Mix the pulsed peas, chickpea flour, caramelised onion, mint, and salt and pepper into the mashed potato.

Warm a layer of olive oil in a large frying pan (skillet) over a medium heat. Using a small ice-cream scoop, or two spoons to form quenelles, gently add the fritters to the frying pan and cook until nice and crispy on each side.

While the fritters are cooking, mix the garlic mayo ingredients together in a bowl and set aside.

Once the fritters are cooked, drain on a piece of paper towel and serve with the garlic mayo and lemon wedges on the side.

MAKE YOUR OWN
TORTILLA FEAST

This is a feast consisting of lots of little elements which once put together creates a party in your mouth. It is an interactive dining experience where every mouthful is the discovery of a new flavour combination.

Note: The Almond Feta [see page 182] should be made the day before because it needs to sit in the fridge overnight.

METHOD

To make the tortillas, whizz up the spinach leaves and water in a food processor or blender to make a green water.

Add the flour to a mixing bowl and make a crater in the middle. Add the spinach water, oil and salt to the crater and work everything together slowly to form a ball of dough, adding a little more flour if it is too sticky. Cut the dough into 12 equal parts and roll into little dough balls.

Place each dough ball on a clean floured surface and roll out as thinly as possible without breaking them. You can either store each tortilla between pieces of greaseproof (waxed) paper to cook later or fry them straightaway.

To cook the tortillas, heat some olive oil in a frying pan (skillet) and cook each tortilla until slightly browned on each side. Keep the tortillas warm under a dish towel as you make them.

To make the refried beans, over a medium heat cook the onion, garlic and spices in some olive oil in a saucepan for 5 minutes until the onions are translucent. Add the beans and water, and turn the heat down to gently simmer. Use a potato masher to mash the beans slightly over the heat, retaining some texture and continuing to stir to prevent sticking.

INGREDIENTS

FOR THE TORTILLAS:

20 g [¾ oz] spinach leaves
180 ml [6 fl oz/¾ cup] water
365 g [12½ oz/2¾ cups] plain (all-purpose) flour, plus extra for dusting
3 tablespoons olive oil, plus extra for frying
pinch of salt

FOR THE REFRIED BEANS:

1 large yellow onion, chopped
2 garlic cloves, finely chopped
pinch of chilli powder
pinch of ground cumin
pinch of coriander seeds
pinch of sweet paprika
olive oil, for frying
2 x 400 g [14 oz] tins of pinto beans or black beans (or 1 of each), drained and rinsed
100 ml [3 ½ fl oz/scant ½ cup] water

FOR THE SUNFLOWER MINCE:

200 g [7 oz] sunflower seeds
1 large yellow onion, chopped
2 garlic cloves, chopped
olive oil, for frying
3 tablespoons tamari or soy sauce
2 tablespoons tomato purée (paste)
1 tablespoon thyme leaves
1 tablespoon oregano leaves
100 g [3½ oz/½ cup] cooked rice (prepared according to the packet directions)

Once the beans are ready, place in a serving dish and top with the coriander leaves and lime wedges on the side.

To make the sunflower mince, pulse the sunflower seeds in a food processor or blender.

Over a medium heat, cook the onion and garlic in some olive oil in a saucepan for a few minutes, then add the pulsed sunflower seeds and the remainder of the ingredients (except for the rice). Fry for a few minutes until everything becomes slightly crispy, then add the cooked rice just before serving and mix together.

To make the salsa, mix all the ingredients together in a bowl until well combined.

To make the pea guacamole, place all the ingredients in a food processor or blender and pulse gently until well mixed but still with some chunky bits.

For the quick pickled onions, soak the sliced onion in the apple cider vinegar and brown sugar as you get everything else to the table.

Serve everything in lovely dishes and platters, including the almond feta, and create a spread in the middle of the table for everyone to build their own tortilla experience! You can use a lettuce leaf to hold the fillings instead of a tortilla, if you wish.

COOK'S TIP:

If you are storing the tortilla dough before cooking, keep it somewhere cool – ideally in the fridge.

SERVES
4–6

FOR THE ALMOND FETA:

1 batch of Almond Feta
   (see page 182)

FOR THE SALSA:

3 tomatoes, diced
½ mango (or any sweet fruit), diced
½ shallot, sliced
1½ tablespoons olive oil
zest and juice of 1 lime
salt and pepper, to taste

FOR THE PEA GUACAMOLE:

125 g (4 oz) frozen peas
½ ripe avocado
¼ fresh chilli, sliced, or a pinch
   of chilli (hot pepper) flakes
juice of ½ lemon
salt and pepper, to taste

FOR THE QUICK PICKLED
ONIONS:

2 red onions, thinly sliced
4–5 tablespoons apple cider vinegar
1 teaspoon soft brown sugar

TO SERVE:

20 g (¾ oz) coriander
   (cilantro) leaves
1 lime, chopped into wedges
baby gem lettuce leaves (optional)

MAKE YOUR OWN KOREAN-STYLE FEAST

I have been to South Korea on a number of occasions over the last 10 years and it is still one of my favourite cuisines. Korean cuisine traditionally consists of many smaller dishes that balance each other out. Spicy, salty, sweet and sour are all elements of a great meal. I have taken inspiration and flavours from my travels when putting this feast together.

SERVES
4–6

METHOD

Preheat the oven to 200°C (400°F/gas 6).

Separate the cauliflower florets and leaves, and chop into bite-size pieces, including the stalk.

In a large bowl, mix the gochujang paste, maple syrup and olive oil to make a dressing. Add all the cauliflower florets and leaves, and coat well with the dressing. If it's a large cauliflower, add more olive oil to the dressing to make sure everything is well covered.

Spread the cauliflower out in a large baking tray (pan) lined with baking parchment. Sprinkle with the sesame seeds and cook in the oven for 45–60 minutes, depending on how crispy you like your cauliflower.

Make the celeriac and apple slaw by mixing all the ingredients together in a bowl, then set aside.

When the cauliflower is ready, remove from the oven and sprinkle with the spring onions.

Cut the nori sheets into four. To do this, fold the nori sheet in half and then in half again, so that you have four scored sections, then cut along the lines with a pair of scissors. The nori sheets and the baby gem lettuce leaves will serve as the perfect vessels for holding the filling.

Now it's time to build your own mouthful! Take a piece of nori (or a lettuce leaf), add some rice, then some cauliflower, slaw and pickles, or your choice of condiment, and pop it all in your mouth.

INGREDIENTS

FOR THE GOCHUJANG
CAULIFLOWER:

1 big cauliflower head
   (leaves and all)
2 tablespoons gochujang paste
   (found in any Asian supermarket)
1 tablespoon maple syrup
2 tablespoons olive oil
4 tablespoons sesame seeds,
   black or white

TOPPING:

1 bunch of spring onions
   (scallions), finely sliced

FOR THE CELERIAC
AND APPLE SLAW:

1 celeriac (celery root),
   peeled and grated
1 apple, peeled, cored and grated
juice of 1 lemon (pour this
   over the apple once grated
   to stop it going brown)
2–3 tablespoons plant mayonnaise
1 tablespoon maple syrup
20 g (¾ oz) chives, snipped
salt and pepper, to taste

TO SERVE:

1 packet of nori sheets
   (you'll need at least 10 sheets)
baby gem lettuce leaves
short-grain steamed rice,
   cooked according to packet
   instructions
Japanese pickles
pickled ginger
kimchi

LIGHT AS A FEATHER TIRAMISÙ

/

Have you heard of aquafaba? It is the leftover chickpea water in a tin of chickpeas, and it is magic. Whip the aquafaba up and it transforms into a white fluff that is the basic ingredient for this feathery light dessert.

SERVES
6–8

○

METHOD

First, make the Vanilla Sponge Cake Base and set aside to cool down.

Meanwhile, whisk the aquafaba in a bowl until it is white, fluffy and forming peaks. This will take around 10 minutes with an electric whisk.

To make a smooth tiramisù cream, blitz the tofu, maple syrup and vanilla in a food processor or blender.

Gently fold the aquafaba mixture into the silken tofu mixture, keeping as much air in as possible. Set aside.

Mix the coffee and Amaretto together in another bowl.

Once the sponge cake has cooled, cut into slices to fit the glass dish you're using for the tiramisù (see also Cook's Tips).

To assemble, cover the bottom of the dish with one layer of tiramisù cream, then add a layer of sponge. Spoon the coffee liquid over the sponge, then keep layering until you have used up all the ingredients, finishing with a layer of whipped cream on top.

Decorate the tiramisù with your choice of toppings and keep in the fridge until ready to serve.

COOK'S TIPS:

- If you don't have a glass serving bowl, make the tiramisù in a glass ovenproof dish or in individual glasses, so you can see the beautiful layers.

- If you are not vegan, you can use classic lady finger biscuits as your sponge element.

INGREDIENTS

1 *Vanilla Sponge Cake Base* (see page 184), baked in a 31 x 37 cm (12 x 14 in) baking tray (pan) as a sheet cake
4 tablespoons aquafaba
350 g (12 oz) firm silken tofu (I prefer organic)
3–4 tablespoons maple syrup (depending on how sweet you like this dessert)
1 vanilla pod (bean), split and the seeds scraped out, or 1 teaspoon vanilla paste or extract
60 ml (2 fl oz/¼ cup) brewed strong coffee, cooled down
2 tablespoons Amaretto
160 ml (5½ fl oz/⅔ cup) whippable plant cream

SUGGESTED TOPPINGS:

shavings of dark chocolate, with 70% cocoa solids
sieved cacao powder
whole coffee beans

PISTACHIO, DATE & CUSTARD FILO PARCELS

/

I am a big custard fan. I also love a quick solution, and this is exactly what this beauty is. Maximum flavour, minimum effort. The parcels can also be easily pre-cooked and eaten cooled.

SERVES
6—8

○

METHOD

If you are making the no-churn ice cream, begin by putting a metal mixing bowl in the fridge for 10 minutes. If not, then skip these next few steps.

Keeping the tins upright, scoop the coconut cream from the tins of coconut cream/milk, reserving the clear liquid for other uses. Add to the chilled mixing bowl.

Using a hand-held mixer, whip the cream until smooth and creamy, then add the sugar and vanilla. Whip until fully incorporated. Ladle the ice cream into a container that is not too deep for the ice cream to set. Add the Medjool dates, cardamom pods and cinnamon to create a nice pattern. Put the ice cream in the freezer to set.

You can remove the ice cream after a couple of hours for a chilled, mousse-like consistency or freeze overnight if you would like a firmer ice cream. You will need to remove the ice cream from the freezer at least 20 minutes before serving and use a scoop warmed under hot water to get a proper scoop. The ice cream will keep in the freezer for up to one week but is best used fresh.

To make the filo parcels, preheat the oven to 180°C (350°F/ gas 4). Grease a oven tray and get on with blitzing the pitted dates, vanilla and pistachios in a food processor or blender until you have a sticky mixture. Take your filo pastry out of the packet and cut the sheets into strips (about 7 cm/3 in thick) lengthwise.

INGREDIENTS

FOR THE FILO PARCELS:

vegan butter or coconut oil,
    for greasing
200 g (7 oz) Medjool dates,
    pitted and torn
1 vanilla pod (bean), split and the
    seeds scraped out, or 1 teaspoon
    vanilla paste or extract
70 g (2½ oz) pistachios
2 packets (about 500 g/1 lb 2 oz)
    of ready-made filo pastry

FOR THE CUSTARD:

double batch of *Homemade Custard*
    (double the recipe on page 183)

FOR THE TOPPING:

30 g (1 oz) vegan butter, melted,
    or coconut oil
1 tablespoon maple syrup
chopped pistachios
2 tablespoons soft brown sugar

FOR THE NO-CHURN ICE CREAM
(OPTIONAL):

3 x 400 g (14 oz) tins of coconut
    cream or full-fat coconut milk,
    chilled in the fridge overnight
3 tablespoons caster (superfine)
    sugar
½ vanilla pod (bean), split and the
    seeds scraped out, or ½ teaspoon
    vanilla paste or extract
4 Medjool dates, pitted and torn
2 cardamom pods, ground in a pestle
    and mortar, or ½ teaspoon
    ground cardamom
1 teaspoon cinnamon

Add a generous layer of custard and a layer of the date and pistachio mix on the right corner of the strip and fold diagonally to the left, enclosing the filling and forming a triangle. Fold again along the upper crease of the triangle. Keep folding in this way until you reach the end of the strip. Brush the outer surface with melted butter.

With a pastry brush, cover the whole of the top layer of pastry with the melted vegan butter/coconut oil, drizzle with maple syrup, then sprinkle with the chopped pistachios and brown sugar and place on the pre-greased oven tray.

Bake in the oven for 30 minutes, until golden brown.

Once the filo parcels are cooked, remove from the oven and serve hot with the no-churn ice-cream (if using), or leave to cool to room temperature before you serve.

SAFFRON PANNA COTTA POTS & POACHED PEARS

/

Saffron reminds me of Sweden and panna cotta is one of my all-time favourite desserts. So why not marry those two together? The poached pear cuts through the creaminess and also adds an additional layer of colour.

MAKES
6 SMALL / 4 LARGE
SERVINGS

○

METHOD

Add the pears to a small saucepan and just cover with poaching liquid. Add the lemon juice, sugar and diced beetroot (the beetroot is purely to give the pears a lovely pink colour once they are cooked).

Simmer for 30 minutes and allow to cool. Slice the pears into quarters lengthways and keep in the fridge until you're ready to serve. You could keep them in the poaching liquid overnight.

To make the panna cotta, add the coconut milk to a pan and heat gently. Add the vanilla, maple syrup and saffron. Then sprinkle the agar agar on top of the liquid and heat through without stirring. Get it to a simmer, whisking let the agar agar dissolve fully. Once the mixture has come to a boil, remove from the heat.

Pour the panna cotta mixture into serving glasses and set aside to cool. Once cooled, place in the fridge to set for a few hours.

Just before serving, place the poached pears on top of each panna cotta and sprinkle with toasted nuts or choice of edible flowers.

COOK'S TIP:

Make this delicious dessert in the morning or the day before, ready to serve in the evening.

INGREDIENTS

FOR THE POACHED PEARS:

2 pears, peeled
poaching liquid (either water
   or white wine)
juice of 1 lemon
5 tablespoons caster (superfine)
   sugar
½ beetroot, peeled and diced,
   or 1 tablespoon beetroot powder

FOR THE PANNA COTTA:

1 litre (34 fl oz/4 cups) coconut milk
1 vanilla pod (bean), split and the
   seeds scraped out, or 1 teaspoon
   vanilla paste or extract
3 tablespoons maple syrup
pinch of saffron
2 tablespoons agar agar

SUGGESTED TOPPINGS:

toasted nuts (such as almonds
   and walnuts)
edible flowers (such as cornflowers,
   nasturtiums and violets)

EASTER AND SPRING

Spring represents the start
of something new: fresh
beginnings, progress, the
blossoming of new things,
birth and plants. Dreaming
of flowers blossoming in
nature and all the incredible
produce it brings. Al fresco
dining, garden gatherings,
picnics in the wild, long walks
and sunshine on our faces
after a long winter. It is one
of my favourite seasons,
filled with light and wonderful
things to come.

GREEN CHICKPEA DIPPERS WITH CHIPOTLE MAYO

These make a great little starter and are the ultimate finger food – a mouthful that is oh-so satisfactory and a taster for things to come. I like wrapping these in baby gem lettuces with a dollop of creamy chipotle for good measure.

Note: The dried chickpeas will need soaking overnight, so bear this in mind when planning this dish.

MAKES
18 DIPPERS

METHOD

Drain and rinse the chickpeas that you soaked overnight.

Blitz all the ingredients for the dippers (except the olive oil) in a food processor or blender until smooth.

Using two large spoons, take 1 tablespoon of the dipper mixture and form into quenelles. Shallow-fry in olive oil in a frying pan (skillet) for a few minutes, turning to brown all sides. Repeat until you have used up all the mixture (about 18 dippers).

To make the chipotle mayo, mix both ingredients in a bowl and set aside.

To serve, separate individual baby gem lettuce leaves and arrange in a single layer on a platter. Place a chickpea dipper on each lettuce leaf and drizzle with the chipotle mayo and Sriracha sauce.

INGREDIENTS

FOR THE DIPPERS:

250 g (9 oz/ 1 cup) dried chickpeas, soaked overnight in a large bowl of water
½ shallot, diced
handful of spinach leaves
1 tablespoon tahini
juice of ½ lemon
2 garlic cloves
pinch of salt
olive oil, for shallow-frying

FOR THE CHIPOTLE MAYO:

200 g (7 oz/¾ cup) plant mayonnaise
1 teaspoon chipotle oil or a pinch of chipotle powder

TO SERVE:

1–2 baby gem lettuce heads
Sriracha sauce

ROASTED BROCCOLI WITH CHEESY POLENTA & CHIVES

Cauliflower has had its moment in the limelight in my book, so now I think it's broccoli's turn to shine. Poached whole with a zingy dressing over creamy polenta, this dish will impress both your eyes and taste buds.

SERVES
4

INGREDIENTS

2 broccoli heads
  (about 800 g/1 lb 12 oz)
1 litre (34 fl oz/4 cups) water
4 tablespoons tamari or soy sauce
2 cm (¾ in) piece of ginger root, grated
2 tablespoons olive oil
2 tablespoons sesame seeds

FOR THE DRESSING:

½ small red onion, chopped
1 tablespoon capers, chopped
1 tablespoon gherkins, chopped
½ apple, chopped
60 ml (2 fl oz/¼ cup) olive oil
1½ tablespoons apple cider vinegar
salt and pepper

FOR THE POLENTA:

160 g (5½ oz/1 cup) polenta
960 ml (32 fl oz/3¾ cups) water
60 ml (2 fl oz/¼ cup) plant cream
30 g (1 oz) chives, finely snipped
1 tablespoon nutritional yeast
salt and pepper, to taste

METHOD

Preheat the oven to 180°C (350°F/gas 4). Line a large baking tray (pan) with baking parchment.

Prepare the broccoli by chopping 1 cm (½ in) from the base of the stem and peeling the rest of the stem. Keep the stem and broccoli head intact. Cut each broccoli head in half through the top and down the stem.

Bring a large saucepan of water to the boil and add the tamari/soy sauce and ginger.

Once boiled, add the four broccoli halves to the pan, blanch for 5 minutes (be careful not to overcook) and then drain.

Lay each broccoli half, flat side down, in the baking tray. Baste with the olive oil and sprinkle with the sesame seeds. Cook in the oven for 10–15 minutes, or until golden brown.

While the broccoli is cooking, mix all the dressing ingredients together in a bowl until well combined. Set aside.

For the polenta, bring a saucepan of water (960 ml/ 32 fl oz/3¾ cups) to the boil and add the polenta. Keep stirring until the mixture starts to thicken. Once thickened, remove from the heat, add the cream, chives, nutritional yeast, and salt and pepper, and mix well.

Serve immediately by adding a big dollop of creamy polenta to each plate and placing half a broccoli head on top. Drizzle generously with the dressing.

CHICKPEA-CRUSTED
SPRING PIE
–PAGE 42–

SPRING CRUDITÉS
& SPICY AÏOLI
–PAGE 44–

HASSLEBACK SWEDE
FILLED WITH ALMOND
FETA & THYME PESTO
—PAGE 45—

CHICKPEA-CRUSTED
SPRING PIE

/

I have made many versions of this beauty. The great thing is that, in theory, it can be filled with any hero vegetable in season.

○

METHOD

Preheat the oven to 180°C (350°F/gas 4). Grease a 24 cm (9½ in) rectangular pie dish, although you can use circular dish with a diameter of 21 cm (8¼ in), if you wish, as pictured.

Start by making the pastry dough for the pie. Add all the flours, the oil, water and salt to a bowl and start mixing everything together to form a dough. Start kneading out all the bumps – you should have a lovely, firm dough ball. Cover with cling film (plastic wrap) and set aside for 15 minutes (not in the fridge).

To make the filling, crumble the tofu into a food processor or blender, then add the remainder of the ingredients. Blitz until smooth and set aside.

Once the dough as rested, place it on a clean floured surface and roll it out with a rolling pin. If necessary, add extra sprinkles of flour to keep the rolling pin from sticking.

Once you have rolled the dough out to the desired size, slowly loosen it up from the work surface ready to transfer to your pie dish.

INGREDIENTS

FOR THE DOUGH:

150 g (5 oz/scant 1 cup) rice flour
150 g (5 oz/1¼ cups) gluten-free flour (or good-quality plain/all-purpose flour if you have no issues with gluten), plus extra for dusting
40 g (1¼ oz/⅓ cup) chickpea (gram) flour
100 ml (3½ fl oz/scant ½ cup) rapeseed or olive oil
145 ml (5 fl oz/scant 1 cup) water
pinch of sea salt

FOR THE FILLING:

600 g (1 lb 5 oz) tofu (I prefer organic)
200 ml (7 fl oz/scant 1 cup) plant milk (I prefer coconut milk)
2 tablespoons flaxseed (whole or ground)
1–2 tablespoons curry powder
2 tablespoons olive oil
salt and pepper, to taste

FOR THE SEASONAL SPRING VEGETABLES:

Use anything in season, but for spring, I suggest:

a handful of asparagus
a handful of kale
a handful of tenderstem broccoli or purple-sprouting broccoli
1 pak choi (bok choi)
a few chicory (endive) leaves
fresh ramps (wild garlic)

Gently lay the rolled dough in the dish and start shaping it against the sides. If there are any gaps, use any leftover bits of dough that you might have in other areas. Press the edges of the dough down gently with a fork and puncture the base so the pastry cooks evenly. Put the pie crust in the oven for 10 minutes to pre-cook before filling it.

While the pie crust is cooking, prepare the spring vegetables by washing thoroughly and patting dry with paper towel. Remove the hard bits from the bottom of the broccoli, asparagus and the pak choi and de-stem the kale. (I like to save the pak choi bottom for the pie as it looks very pretty.)

Heat some olive oil in a frying pan (skillet) and lightly fry all the vegetables on one side. Be careful not to let them get too brown and then gently turn to the other side. Once cooked, set aside until assembly.

Once the pie crust is light brown, it is ready to be filled with the tofu filling and vegetables. Pour the filling in first, evening it out and giving an extra seasoning of salt and pepper.

Add the half-cooked vegetables, arranging them beautifully and pushing them down slightly into the filling (especially the fragrant ramps).

Once everything is in the pie casing, bake in the oven for 20–25 minutes until the filling is firm and the vegetables are golden brown.

Sprinkle with some extra chopped chilli, if you wish, and serve with a big salad.

SERVES
6–8

TO SERVE:

½ fresh red chilli,
    chopped (optional)
large leafy green salad

SPRING CRUDITÉS
& SPICY AÏOLI

This dish is a homage to spring produce.
You can build an array of produce around
a spicy aïoli that will transform even the
humblest of vegetables.

SERVES
4–6

INGREDIENTS

3 tablespoons aquafaba
   (liquid from tinned chickpeas)
1 tablespoon apple cider vinegar
½ teaspoon Dijon mustard
240 ml (8½ fl oz/1 cup) vegetable oil
juice of 1 lemon
2 garlic cloves, chopped
pinch of saffron
salt and pepper, to taste

FOR THE RAW VEGETABLES:

radish
carrots
cucumber
chicory (endive)
fennel
celery stalks

METHOD

Combine the aquafaba, apple cider vinegar, mustard,
and salt and pepper in a bowl using a hand-held whisk.

Slowly add the oil while whisking with an electric whisk
until it emulsifies into a lovely mayonnaise consistency.

Then add the lemon juice, garlic and saffron and whisk
again until everything is well combined.

Chop the raw vegetables into bite-size pieces and arrange
on a serving tray, ready for dipping!

HASSLEBACK SWEDE FILLED WITH ALMOND FETA & THYME PESTO

Let's bring the swede (rutabaga) back. When cooked well, it deserves to be centre stage. Here it needs to be slow-roasted and then filled with incredible crumbly almond feta to jazz it up. Let's give the swede the praise it deserves.

Note: The Almond Feta (see page 182) should be made the day before because it needs to sit in the fridge overnight.

INGREDIENTS

2 swedes (rutabagas), peeled
2–3 tablespoons olive oil
2 handfuls of kale, cavolo nero
    or chard (or a mixture),
    roughly chopped
pinch of salt
handful of rocket (arugula), to serve

FOR THE ALMOND FETA:

Almond Feta (see page 182)
10g (½ oz) thyme leaves, chopped
1 teaspoon nutritional yeast
zest of ½ lemon
1 garlic clove, grated
pinch of salt and pepper

FOR THE GREEN PESTO:

100 g (3½ oz) sunflower seeds
30 g (1 oz) basil leaves
10 g (½ oz) thyme leaves
10 g (½ oz) mint leaves
100 ml (3½ fl oz/⅓ cup) olive oil
1 garlic clove
salt and pepper, to taste

METHOD

Preheat the oven to 200°C (400°F/gas 6).

Cut the swedes in half and hassleback each half by slicing across the swede every 5 mm (¼ in) almost to the bottom, but not cutting through the base. Then slice in half again lengthways.

Add the swedes to a baking tray (pan), pour over some olive oil and cook in the oven for 1 hour, or until they are nicely browned and have opened slightly.

Massage the greens with some olive oil, sprinkle with salt and arrange around the swedes in the baking tray. Cook for a further 10 minutes.

Mix the almond feta ingredients together in a bowl, add to a piping bag and then pipe between each of the slices of the hasselbacked swedes.

Blitz all the green pesto ingredients together in a food processor or blender.

To serve, drizzle the pesto over the swedes and feta, then scatter over the rocket.

MACADAMIA NUT CHEESE-FILLED COURGETTE FLOWERS

This has become such a classic. I love cooking these filled flowers for events or dinner parties. Courgette (zucchini) flowers are stunning and make the perfect vessels for a variety of delicious fillings.

Note: You will need to make the Garlic & Herb Macadamia Cheese (see page 128) for this recipe the day before.

METHOD

Put the cheese mixture in a piping (pastry) bag, fill the courgette flowers two-thirds full and gently twist the tops to close them up.

Once the flowers have been filled, make the batter by mixing all the ingredients together.

Heat a good amount of olive oil in a saucepan. Gently dip the courgette flowers in the batter and then shallow-fry over a medium heat until browned. Make sure you fry off each side of the flowers until they are nice and crispy.

Once fried, place the flowers on a paper towel to get rid of excess oil and serve immediately with some spring greens and a lemon-flavoured mayonnaise with a few snipped chives stirred in.

INGREDIENTS

8 courgette (zucchini) flowers
1 batch of *Garlic & Herb Macadamia Cheese* (see page 128)
olive oil, for frying

FOR THE BATTER:

50 g (2 oz/⅓ cup) cornflour (cornstarch)
35 g (1¼ oz/¼ cup) plain (all-purpose) flour or rice flour, for a gluten-free version
2 tablespoons chickpea (gram) flour
1 teaspoon baking powder
120 ml (4 fl oz/½ cup) sparkling water

TO SERVE:

spring greens
lemon-flavoured mayonnaise
snipped chives

ALMOND GALETTE
WITH CREAM & APRICOTS

An impressive yet very easy dessert to make ahead of time. Make the galette beforehand so all you have to do is put it together and make a lasting impression.

SERVES
4–6

METHOD:

Preheat the oven to 180°C (350°F/gas 4). Line a large baking tray (pan) with baking parchment.

Mix the ingredients for the galette together in a food processor to combine well until it has a sticky consistency. Place the dough between two pieces of greaseproof (waxed) paper and roll out until it is 1 cm (½ in) thick and about 20–25 cm (8–10 in) in diameter.

Remove the top layer of greaseproof paper from the galette and place on an oven tray. Bake in the oven for 15 minutes until golden. Remove from the oven and leave to cool. When cool, place the greaseproof paper on a serving plate and cut around it so as not to break the pastry.

Mix all of the topping ingredients (except the apricots) in a bowl and then spread the mixture over the cooled galette.

Thinly slice the apricots into half-moons and arrange over the topping, then scatter with almonds.

COOK'S TIP:

Put the components of this dish together just before serving to keep it nice and fresh.

INGREDIENTS

FOR THE GALETTE:

120 g (4 oz/1¼ cups) almond flour
120 g (4 oz/1 cup) buckwheat flour
60 g (2 oz/⅓ cup) soft brown sugar
zest of 1 lemon or lime
120 ml (4 fl oz/½ cup) grapeseed oil
   (or any flavourless oil)

FOR THE TOPPING:

200 g (7 oz/scant 1 cup) oat-based crème fraîche, coconut whipped cream (see page 187) or plant yoghurt
zest of 1 lime
1 vanilla pod (bean), split and the seeds scraped out, or 1 teaspoon vanilla paste or extract
1 tablespoon maple syrup
3–4 apricots, pitted
handful of almonds, chopped

BREAD & BUTTER PUDDING WITH ROASTED VANILLA RHUBARB & CUSTARD

Do you have leftover stale bread lying around? I know exactly what you can make with it. Reimagined bread and butter pudding with rhubarb and custard. So good!

INGREDIENTS

FOR THE PUDDING:

500 ml (17 fl oz/2 cups) coconut milk
100 g (3½ oz) pitted dates
1 teaspoon cinnamon
½ teaspoon ground cloves
½ teaspoon ground cardamom
1 baguette or 500 g (1 lb 2 oz) stale
    bread (preferably white)

FOR THE ROASTED RHUBARB:

380 g (13 oz) fresh rhubarb
zest of 1 orange
½ vanilla pod (bean), split and the
    seeds scraped out, or ½ teaspoon
    vanilla paste or extract
2 tablespoons maple syrup

FOR THE CUSTARD:

1 batch of *Homemade Custard*
    (see page 183)

METHOD

Whizz the coconut milk, dates, cinnamon, cloves and cardamom in a food processor or blender until smooth.

Tear the bread into a deep baking dish, then pour the coconut milk mixture over the top. Let the mixture soak into the bread for at least 1 hour, or overnight.

When you are ready to bake the pudding, preheat the oven to 180°C (350°F/gas 4) and bake for 45 minutes.

Meanwhile, make the roasted rhubarb by cutting each stalk into three pieces. Add to a bowl with the orange zest, vanilla and maple syrup. Mix well to coat the rhubarb.

Line a baking tray (pan) with baking parchment and add the marinated rhubarb, pouring any remaining marinade on top. Roast in the oven for 30 minutes once the pudding has been baking for 15 minutes, so they are both ready at the same time.

While the bread and butter pudding is cooking, make the custard.

Serve the bread and butter pudding with the roasted rhubarb and some Homemade Custard on the side.

CHOCOLATE
PULL-APART BREAD

/

An Easter bread with a difference.
It contains chocolate, tick, and is sticky
and sweet, double tick. Great to make
as a family or with kids, and it also
makes a lovely gift.

MAKES
1 LOAF

INGREDIENTS

180 ml (6 fl oz/generous ½ cup)
  plant milk
80 g (3 oz) vegan butter
25 g (1 oz) fresh yeast or 2 teaspoons
  fast-action dry yeast
4 teaspoons soft brown sugar
440 g (1 lb/2 cups) plain
  (all-purpose) flour
pinch of salt

FOR THE FILLING:

60 g (2 oz) hazelnuts
50 g (2 oz) vegan butter
90 g (3½ oz/½ cup) soft brown sugar
1 teaspoon ground cinnamon
1 teaspoon ground cardamom
½ teaspoon ground cloves
100 g (3½ oz) chocolate chips
  or chopped chocolate (optional)

FOR THE ICING:

100 g (3½ oz/¾ cup) icing
  (confectioner's) sugar
1 tablespoon maple syrup
1 tablespoon vegan butter, melted
½ vanilla pod (bean), split and the
  seeds scraped out, or ½ teaspoon
  vanilla paste or extract

○

METHOD

Gently heat the milk and butter in a saucepan over a low
heat. Remove from the heat and leave to cool down until the
mixture is warm but not piping hot. A good way to test this is
to dip your finger in the mixture – it should be warm but not
burning. This ensures that the fresh yeast (if using) is
activated and that will dissolve.

Once the mixture reaches a warm temperature, add the
yeast and mix well. Then stir in the sugar and pinch of salt
until fully dissolved.

Transfer this mixture to a bowl and add the flour. Mix
everything together well and then use the heel of your hand
to knead until a nice dough ball is formed.

Once the dough has been worked and is slightly springy,
leave in the bowl, cover with a dish towel and keep
somewhere warm to rise for at least 1 hour to 1 hour
30 minutes.

While the bread is rising, make the filling by heating the
hazelnuts in a saucepan until they start to toast. Once
toasted, remove from the pan and set aside.

Add the butter and sugar to the same pan and heat until
the butter melts and the sugar dissolves. Stir in the spices
and remove from the heat.

Line a large loaf pan with baking parchment and arrange a
handful of hazelnuts over the bottom along with a spoonful
or two of the butter-sugar mixture.

Now arrange the dough. Cut the dough in half and then in half again until you have 16 bigger pieces or 32 smaller ones. Roll the pieces into balls and dip them in the remaining butter-sugar mixture.

Start building the balls up in the loaf pan, adding some chocolate chips and the rest of the hazelnuts between the layers of balls. Don't squish the balls or worry about any gaps as those will be filled when the dough rises again. Cover with a dish towel and leave to prove for 30 minutes.

Preheat the oven to 180°C [350°F/gas 4].

Bake the bread for 30–45 minutes until golden brown. Once baked, allow to cool in the pan on a wire rack and turn out once cooled.

Mix the ingredients for the icing together in a bowl and drizzle over the bread once it has cooled down completely.

CHOCOLATE & HONEYCOMB BRITTLE BARK

Honeycomb is the best, especially when it's drizzled with chocolate and sprinkled with chopped nuts. We are going the extra mile with these and making them very giftable. Or you can just keep them all to yourself.

MAKES
1 TRAY

INGREDIENTS

125 g (4 oz) golden (corn) syrup
200 g (7 oz) sugar
2 tablespoons water
2 teaspoons bicarbonate of soda (baking soda)
2 bars of vegan milk or dark chocolate

SUGGESTED TOPPINGS:

dried fruits (such as raisins, currants and figs)
nuts (such as hazelnuts, pecans, pistachios, cashews and flaked/slivered almonds)
dried flower petals (such as cornflowers)

METHOD

Heat the golden syrup, sugar and water in a very large saucepan, stirring occasionally until golden brown. If you have a sugar thermometer, the liquid is ready when it reaches 150°C (300°F). If you don't have a thermometer, drop some of the mixture into cold water – if it hardens quickly and cracks, it is ready; if it is mouldable and bendy, it needs to boil a bit longer.

Line a baking tray (pan) with greaseproof (waxed) paper.

When the sugar liquid is ready, remove from the heat and add the bicarbonate of soda and stir well. The mixture will go white and bubbly and double in size (which is why it is very important to use a large pan!).

Pour the mixture onto the lined baking tray and place in the fridge to harden.

Meanwhile, melt the chocolate in a bain-marie and pour over the hardened honeycomb. Add your choice of toppings immediately before the chocolate starts to harden.

Return to the fridge and once the honeycomb is fully set, break into pieces and put in bags as gifts, or simply eat them yourself!

COOK'S TIP:

If you have any leftover chocolate bars, this is a good way to use them up.

CHOCOLATE EGGS & SWEET FILLINGS

I bet you already have most of these ingredients in your storecupboard. I make these with my daughter every year and we vary the fillings according to how adventurous she is feeling. You will need an egg mould for this recipe, which you can find online or at some large supermarkets.

MAKES
1 LARGE EGG OR
6–8 SMALLER
EGGS

INGREDIENTS

200 g (7 oz) coconut oil
6 tablespoons maple syrup or honey
125 g (4 oz/1 cup) cacao powder

FOR THE SALTED DATE CARAMEL:

16 Medjool dates, pitted
60 ml (2 fl oz/¼ cup) soaking water
  (from the dates)
½ teaspoon vanilla extract
1 tablespoon nut butter
pinch of salt

SUGGESTED FILLINGS:

Lotus Biscoff spread
peanut butter
almond butter
jam
Nutella

METHOD

Before making the eggs, soften the dates for the salted caramel by soaking them in a bowl of warm water for about 1 hour. Drain.

Melt the coconut oil in a bain-marie (or in a bowl set over a saucepan of simmering water). Once melted, carefully transfer the bowl to your work surface.

Mix the maple syrup/honey into the melted coconut oil. Then stir in the cacao powder until you have a smooth, liquid chocolate.

Reserving a little of the chocolate mixture, pour the rest into your moulds of choice, tilting these so the mixture covers the surface evenly.

Leave the moulds in the fridge or freezer for around 20 minutes, or until the chocolate has set.

To make the salted date caramel, blitz the softened dates with all the other ingredients in a food processor or blender until everything is well incorporated.

Add the mixture to a piping bag for ease or just use a small spoon when you add the mixture to the Easter eggs. Remove the moulds from the fridge and carefully separate the egg halves. Spoon in the salted caramel and your choice of other fillings.

Brush the rim of each mould with the leftover liquid chocolate, then stick the halves together.

Leave the chocolate eggs to set in the fridge for a further 10 minutes, then enjoy!

BARBECUES & GARDEN PARTIES

There is nothing more enjoyable than standing outside in the garden with the people you love and cooking delicious food. Charring brings an extra layer of texture and flavour to food, not to mention cooking with fire is prehistoric and brings a warm feeling of togetherness. All the elements that, as I write this book during the pandemic, we are all much in need of.

SALMOREJO

Salmorejo is the sibling of gazpacho, but thicker and served with different toppings. It is one of my absolute favourite dishes and this is my own version.

SERVES
4

METHOD

Whizz all the ingredients for the soup in a food processor or blender until well combined. Keep in the fridge or serve immediately.

When you are ready to serve, pour into beautiful serving bowls.

Place the diced toppings in small pots for each person to scatter over their own portion of soup.

Drizzle the salmorejo with olive oil and add a few basil leaves for good measure.

COOK'S TIP:

I would suggest dicing the toppings precisely as it brings a nice visual to a very simple dish.

INGREDIENTS

1 kg (2 lb 4 oz) vine-ripened tomatoes
200 g (7 oz) stale/rustic bread
60 ml (2 fl oz/¼ cup) olive oil
2 garlic cloves
1 tablespoon maple syrup
1–2 teaspoons apple cider vinegar
salt and pepper, to taste

SUGGESTED TOPPINGS:

red onion, finely diced
cucumber, finely diced
avocado, finely diced
extra-virgin olive oil, to drizzle
a few basil leaves

BABY POTATO, COURGETTE & RED ONION SKEWERS WITH HERBED YOGHURT DIP

MAKES
6

I love the combination of new potatoes, courgettes (zucchini) and onion in this recipe. This barbecue dish is very easy to put together to celebrate any occasion. It's also practical because you can simply pre-prepare it at home and bring it along to a gathering!

METHOD

Prepare and heat up the barbecue.

To make the green basting oil, blitz all the ingredients in a food processor or blender until well mixed.

Chop the courgette into slices that are the same width as the baby potatoes.

Push the vegetables onto skewers, alternating the courgette slices with the wedges of red onion and potatoes.

Using a basting brush, baste the skewers with the green oil, covering each side, then cook on the barbecue for 10–15 minutes, or until the potatoes are cooked through. Keep basting the skewers with the remainder of the green oil while they are still on the barbecue, turning occasionally.

While the skewers are cooking, mix all the ingredients for the herbed yoghurt dip together in a bowl and set aside.

Once the skewers are ready, serve with the herbed yoghurt dip on the side.

INGREDIENTS

500 g (1 lb 2 oz) baby pearl potatoes
1 large courgette (zucchini)
1 red onion, cut into quarters

FOR THE GREEN BASTING OIL:

60 ml (2 fl oz/¼ cup) olive oil
30 g (1 oz) flat-leaf parsley leaves, chopped
1 garlic clove
pinch of salt

FOR THE HERBED YOGHURT DIP:

200 g (7 oz/scant 1 cup) plant yoghurt
1 tablespoon plant mayonnaise
1 tablespoon chopped mint leaves
1 tablespoon chopped flat-leaf parsley leaves
½ small shallot, finely chopped
zest and juice of 1 lime
pinch of salt and pepper

CHARRED AUBERGINES & PINEAPPLE SALSA

Whether you love or hate aubergines (eggplants), this is the way to eat them. Scoring the aubergines allows the marinade to cover all surfaces and the pineapple salsa just makes this dish sing!

SERVES 6–8
AS A SIDE DISH

METHOD

Prepare and heat up the barbecue.

Cut the aubergines into quarters lengthways, then use a sharp knife to score across the flesh widthways every 5 mm (¼ in), without cutting through the skin, to create a 'hedgehog' effect.

Rub salt all over the aubergines, then set aside for 30 minutes while you prepare everything else. You will notice that the salt draws liquid from the flesh.

Meanwhile, mix all the marinade ingredients together in a bowl until well combined. Set aside.

Next make the pineapple salsa by chopping the pineapple into very small cubes and adding to a bowl. Mix in the onion, coriander, lime juice, chilli, olive oil and salt, and then set aside.

After 30 minutes, wash or brush the salt from the aubergines, then pour the marinade over them, making sure it covers all the flesh, including right inside the scored areas.

Cook the aubergines on the barbecue for about 10–15 minutes until they are nicely charred on the outside and soft on the inside.

Serve with the pineapple salsa on the side.

INGREDIENTS

2 large aubergines (eggplants)
salt

FOR THE MARINADE:

60 ml (2 fl oz/¼ cup) tamari
   or soy sauce
1 tablespoon tomato ketchup
1 tablespoon honey or maple syrup
1 tablespoon olive oil
1 teaspoon garlic powder
pinch of chilli (hot pepper) flakes

FOR THE PINEAPPLE SALSA:

½ small to medium pineapple,
   skin and core removed
½ red onion, cubed
30 g (1 oz) coriander (cilantro)
   leaves, chopped
juice of 1 lime
½ fresh red chilli, finely chopped
2 tablespoons olive oil
pinch of salt

SUMMER GREENS FILO PIE

This is great for incorporating lots of greens into your diet in the most delicious way possible. The crispy outer layer of filo and the green and good-for-you filling are equally delicious.

SERVES
4–6

METHOD

Preheat the oven to 180°C (350°F/gas 4).

Add the chopped broccoli to a food processor, and blitz down to create a broccoli pulp.

Fry the leek in 2 tablespoons of the olive oil in a large frying pan (skillet) over a medium heat. After 5–10 minutes, or once the leeks have softened, add the garlic and cook for a further few minutes. Then add the broccoli pulp, all the spices and the salt and pepper, and cook for a further 5 minutes.

Fold in the spinach leaves, chickpeas and plant cream, then mix well.

Drizzle the remaining 2 tablespoons of olive oil over the base of a large baking tray (pan) or ovenproof dish.

Add three sheets of filo pastry to the dish, layering them so that some of the sides hang over the edge. Spread half the greens mixture across the top of the pastry. Add another layer of three sheets followed by the remainder of the greens mix.

Place the last sheet of pastry on top and fold in the overhanging edges to create a crust around the edge of the tray/dish.

Use a fork to prick holes all over the pastry, then brush the top and edges with olive oil and maple syrup (don't miss any filo out!) and sprinkle with the nigella seeds.

Bake in the oven for 40 minutes until piping hot with a nice, golden brown crust.

INGREDIENTS

1 broccoli head, roughly chopped
1 large leek, washed thoroughly
    between the layers and
    roughly chopped
60 ml (2 fl oz/¼ cup) olive oil
1 garlic clove, roughly chopped
1 teaspoon ground turmeric
1 teaspoon ground cumin
1 teaspoon mustard seeds
seeds of 3 cardamom pods
    or ½ teaspoon ground cardamom
pinch of ground cinnamon
1 tablespoon salt
pinch of pepper
240 g (8½ oz) spinach leaves
400 g (14 oz) tin chickpeas,
    rinsed and drained
250 ml (8½ fl oz/1 cup) plant cream
    (I like oat cream)
7 sheets (about 270 g/9½ oz)
    of ready-rolled filo pastry

FOR THE TOPPING:

1–2 tablespoons olive oil
1 tablespoon maple syrup
1 tablespoon nigella seeds

BARBECUE LETTUCE & LEEKS WITH GARLIC DRESSING

SERVES
4

Lettuce is one of those ingredients that many people think you can only have in salads. I beg to differ and enjoyed a similar dish in Southern Spain when I lived there for 12 years. The garlic dressing just makes the dish here.

INGREDIENTS

6 heads baby gem lettuce, halved
2 large leeks, washed thoroughly between the layers and halved lengthways

FOR THE GARLIC DRESSING:

60 ml (2 fl oz/¼ cup) olive oil
3 garlic cloves, grated
½ fresh chilli, finely chopped
1 tablespoon sweet paprika powder
zest and juice of 1 lemon
salt and pepper, to taste

METHOD

Prepare and heat up the barbecue.

While waiting for the barbecue to heat up, make the dressing. Heat the olive oil in a frying pan (skillet) over a medium heat, then remove from the heat and add the remainder of the ingredients. They will infuse in the residual heat. Set aside.

Put the lettuce and the leeks, flat-side down first, on the barbecue and cook on both sides until nicely charred.

Serve with the dressing drizzled over the top.

CHARGRILLED SUMMER VEGETABLES WITH CAESAR DRESSING

/

This is an all-in-one charred salad. The best way to incorporate as many hero vegetables as possible is to barbecue them and pair them with a killer dressing.

○

METHOD

Start preparing the Caesar dressing first by soaking the cashew nuts in a bowl of water for 2 hours (you could do this the night before to get ahead).

Place all the prepared vegetables in a large bowl. Mix through the olive oil, maple syrup, chilli powder, and salt and pepper. Make sure all the vegetables are properly coated, then set aside for a few minutes.

Mix all the dressing ingredients (except the capers) in a food processor or blender until super smooth. You should have a super-creamy dressing. Transfer to a small bowl.

Add the chopped capers to the dressing and mix in well, seasoning with more salt and pepper if needed.

Prepare and heat up the barbecue and get all the vegetables on there. Start with the carrots, as they will take slightly longer to cook than the other vegetables. Add the remainder of the vegetables as soon as there is some char on the carrots and then grill until everything is nicely cooked.

To make the croutons, rub the slices of bread with the garlic clove, drizzle with some olive oil and toast on the barbecue, so they will be nice and crisp and give the salad that perfect 'crunch' factor. Chop the bread into bite-size pieces.

Arrange the vegetables beautifully on a serving platter, drizzle generously with the Caesar dressing and sprinkle over the croutons.

INGREDIENTS

2 carrots, cut horizontally
    into 5 mm (¼ in) strips
2 courgettes (zucchini),
    cut horizontally into
    5 mm (¼ in) strips
1 aubergine (eggplant),
    cut horizontally into
    5 mm (¼ in) strips
3 shallots, peeled and
    cut horizontally
300–400 g (10½–14 oz)
    tenderstem broccoli
2 corn on the cob
5 tablespoons olive oil
1 teaspoon maple syrup
½ teaspoon chilli powder
1 teaspoon salt
pinch of pepper

FOR THE CAESAR DRESSING:

100 g (3½ oz) cashew nuts
150 ml (5½ fl oz/generous ½ cup)
    water
1 garlic clove, grated
1 sheet or a few sprigs of dulse
    (about 10 g/½ oz), chopped
zest of 1 lemon, plus a squeeze
    of the juice
1 tablespoon capers, chopped
salt and pepper, to taste

FOR CHARRED CROUTONS:

2–3 slices of bread
1 garlic clove, cut in half,
    for rubbing
olive oil, to drizzle

STICKY GLAZED
MUSHROOM SKEWERS
& GREEN CHIMICHURRI
—PAGE 75—

WHOLE BARBECUE
SPICED GINGER
TOFU & GREENS
—PAGE 74—

WHOLE BARBECUE GINGER SPICED TOFU & GREENS

I have always wanted to barbecue a whole tofu. There is something about a crispy outer layer with a warm soft middle that is very yummy and satisfying. The tofu lies on top of a bed of charred greens and is married with an epic dressing.

METHOD

Drain the tofu and pat dry with some paper towel. Make sure you soak up all the liquid and that the tofu is as dry as possible. I sometimes leave the tofu on a paper towel and then turn it over after 30 minutes or so.

Mix all the marinade ingredients together in a bowl, then add the tofu to marinate it whole. Once your barbecue is fired up, baste the tofu with the marinade using a basting brush. Make sure the tofu is covered all over. You can also marinate it the day before.

Grill the tofu on the barbecue for 6–7 minutes on each side, occasionally brushing with extra marinade. The tofu is done when it looks nicely grilled and is crispy on the outside.

While the tofu is cooking (or you can do this in advance), make the almond topping and the dressing. For the topping, fry the almonds in the olive oil for a few minutes, then add the tamari/soy sauce at the last minute.

To make the dressing, mix all the ingredients (except the sesame seeds) in a bowl until well combined.

A couple of minutes before the tofu is ready, mix the pak choi, baby corn and mangetout in any remaining marinade and add to the barbecue to quickly char. If the pak choi are too big, cut them in half. Barbecue for a few minutes and then set aside.

Remove the tofu and vegetables from the barbecue and create a bed of pak choi, baby corn and mangetout on a serving plate. Slice the tofu and arrange on top.

Sprinkle with the fried almonds and sesame seeds, and drizzle with the dressing. Serve immediately.

SERVES
4–6

INGREDIENTS

400 g (14 oz) firm tofu
   (I prefer organic)
4 pak choi (bok choi)
200 g (7 oz) baby corn
200 g (7 oz) mangetout
   (snow peas)

FOR THE TOFU MARINADE:

3 tablespoons tamari
   or strong soy sauce
1 teaspoon soft brown sugar
1 teaspoon Dijon mustard
1 tablespoon maple syrup
1 tablespoon barbecue spice
1 garlic clove, finely grated
   (optional)
2.5 cm (1 in) piece of ginger
   root, peeled and finely
   grated (optional)

FOR THE ALMOND TOPPING:

100 g (3½ oz) almonds
1 tablespoon olive oil
1 tablespoon tamari
   or strong soy sauce

FOR THE DRESSING:

60 ml (2 fl oz/¼ cup)
   grapeseed oil
2 tablespoons tamari
   or strong soy sauce
1 tablespoon sesame oil
1 teaspoon soft brown sugar
1 garlic clove, grated
a thumbnail-size piece
   of ginger root, peeled
   and grated
sesame seeds, for topping

STICKY GLAZED MUSHROOM SKEWERS & GREEN CHIMICHURRI

I love a good charring and that is exactly what these skewers need. Sticky and chewy on the outside with a sweet soft inside. Drenched in a dreamy green chimichurri, these are heaven on a plate and well worth the process.

METHOD

Mix all the ingredients for the marinade in a bowl.

Place the mushrooms (including the stems) in a large bowl and cover with the marinade. Mix well and leave to marinate for at least 1 hour, or overnight if you have time.

While the mushrooms are marinating, make the chimichurri by mixing all the ingredients together in a bowl before setting aside.

When ready to cook, prepare and heat up the barbecue, then push the mushrooms onto skewers, packing them together very tightly.

Place the skewers on the barbecue and cook for 10 minutes, or until nicely charred, turning them occasionally.

Once the skewers are ready, serve with the chimichurri drizzled over the skewers, or on the side.

MAKES
4–6

INGREDIENTS

500 g (1 lb 2 oz) portobello
  mushrooms, cleaned and cut
  into quarters
500 g (1 lb 2 oz) button mushrooms,
  cleaned, de-stemmed and
  left whole

FOR THE MARINADE:

120 ml (4 fl oz/½ cup) teriyaki sauce
60 ml (2 fl oz/¼ cup) maple syrup
60 ml (2 fl oz/¼ cup) olive oil
2 tablespoons barbecue spice
2 tablespoons Dijon mustard
2 tablespoons Marmite
  (or any yeast extract)

FOR THE CHIMICHURRI:

1 tomato, finely diced
½ red onion, diced
30 g (1 oz) coriander (cilantro)
  leaves, chopped
30 g (1 oz) flat-leaf parsley leaves,
  chopped
30 g (1 oz) basil leaves, chopped
juice of 1 lime
½ fresh red chilli, finely chopped
2 tablespoons olive oil
pinch of salt

BARBECUE WATERMELON & LIME WITH ALMOND FETA

This salad reminds me of summers spent in Bulgaria. Watermelon and feta were a permanent summer fixture there. Here I have combined both in a scrumptious way.

Note: The Almond Feta (see page 182) should be made the day before because it needs to sit in the fridge overnight.

SERVES
4

INGREDIENTS

1 watermelon, cut into quarters
olive oil, to drizzle
2 limes, halved
80 g (2¾ oz) watercress
salt and pepper, to taste

FOR THE ALMOND FETA:

1 batch of *Almond Feta*
   (see page 182)

FOR THE TOPPING:

a few mint leaves
a handful of pomegranate seeds

METHOD

Prepare and heat up the barbecue until it is very hot.

Slice the watermelon into 4–6 triangular slices (I like to keep the rind on). Drizzle the slices with oil on both sides and cook on the barbecue for 3 minutes, or until charred. Grill the lime halves at the same time. Remove the watermelon and limes, then arrange the watermelon on a serving platter over a bed of watercress and set the limes to one side.

Crumble the almond feta over the watermelon, add a few mint leaves and pomegranate seeds, drizzle with more olive oil and season to taste. Squeeze the lime halves over the top and serve.

MY GRANDMA'S
BERRY & CREAM CAKE

/

I remember my Norwegian grandmother making this cake for special occasions. It is time-consuming and slightly intricate, but so worth it. I almost think it tastes better after a day as the ingredients have had a chance to settle. This is a big celebratory cake shared by many!

METHOD

Preheat the oven to 180°C (350°F/gas 4). Grease two 31 x 37 cm (12 x 14 in) rectangular baking trays (pans) with butter (you can also use coconut oil). If you want a smaller cake then half the recipe, and if you only have one tin, you can make this in two batches.

To make the cake, cream the butter and sugar together in a large bowl until soft and fluffy.

In another bowl, whisk the aquafaba until it is white, fluffy and forming stiff peaks. This will take a good 10 minutes. I find an electric whisk makes this much easier! Set aside.

Add the flour, baking powder, milk, apple cider vinegar, vanilla, and salt to the large bowl. Mix to incorporate everything well.

Gently fold the aquafaba through the mix, then pour into the prepared baking trays. I add a sheet of parchment paper so that I can easily pop the cake out and cook the other half (great if you only have one rectangular pan). Bake the cake in the oven for 30–40 minutes.

While the cakes are cooking, make the custard and cream. Simply whip the cream in a bowl, mix in the vanilla and sugar, and set aside. Make the custard in plenty of time so that it is fully cooled when you use it.

Check if the cakes are ready by inserting a skewer into the middle of each and seeing if it comes out clean (it may need an extra 5–10 minutes).

SERVES
12–16

INGREDIENTS

FOR THE CAKE:

300 g (10 oz) vegan butter,
    plus extra for greasing
375 g (13¼ oz/scant 1 cup) caster
    (superfine) sugar (caster sugar
    keeps the cake light and airy)
7½ tablespoons aquafaba
    (liquid from tinned chickpeas)
600 g (1 lb 5 oz/4 cups)
    self-raising flour
2 teaspoons baking powder
500 ml (14 fl oz/2 cups)
    plant milk (I like oat milk)
1 tablespoon apple cider vinegar
1 vanilla pod (bean), split and the
    seeds scraped out, or 1 teaspoon
    vanilla paste or extract
pinch of salt

FOR THE CUSTARD:

2 batches of *Homemade Custard*
    (see page 183).

FOR THE CREAM:

675 ml (23 fl oz/generous 3 cups)
    whippable plant cream
    (I like oat cream)
1 vanilla pod (bean), split and the
    seeds scraped out, or 1 teaspoon
    vanilla paste or extract
2 teaspoons caster (superfine) sugar

Remove the cakes from the oven and place on a wire rack to cool completely. Once fully cooled, pop the cakes out of the pan.

You should have two rectangular cakes, one as the bottom layer and one as the top. Place the bottom cake on a serving platter and spread with a layer of jam followed by a layer of custard, then one of strawberries from one punnet. Add the other cake on top and add another layer of jam – the rougher surface will absorb more jam!

Add the cream to a piping bag (if you have one), then pipe up and down the sides of the cake. Alternatively, use a palette knife to spread the cream over the cake.

Decorate the top of the cake with the halved strawberries from the other punnet, to cover the jam.

Keep the cake in the fridge until ready to serve.

FOR THE FILLING:

1 jar of strawberry jam
    (about 340 g/12 oz)
2 punnets (trays) of strawberries
    (about 200 g/7 oz), de-stemmed
    and halved (one punnet for inside
    the cake and one for the topping)

PAVLOVA WREATH WITH LIME CREAM & SEASONAL FRUITS

SERVES
4–6

A brilliant and pretty dish to serve either as individual nests or a big, impressive wreath. Topped off with seasonal fruits and a tart cream, it is heaven. The instructions here are for one large wreath, but there will be enough mixture to make a nest each for four to six people.

METHOD

Preheat the oven to 110°C (230°F/gas ¼). Using a cake pan or something similar, draw a circle on a piece of baking parchment. Then draw a smaller circle inside to create a ring – about 10 cm (4 in) wide – to make the pavlova wreath. Place the piece of parchment on a baking sheet.

To make the pavlova wreath, whip the aquafaba in a bowl with an electric whisk until stiff peaks form – this will take around 10–20 minutes.

Add the sugar very gradually. Slowly add the cornflour and cream of tartar, ensuring everything is mixed together well. The mixture needs to be stiff and also have a lovely white sheen.

Spoon the mixture onto the ring drawn on the baking parchment. Make a shallow trench in the ring to hold the cream and fruit.

Bake the pavlova in the oven for 1½–2 hours until completely cooked/dried out. Remove from the oven and allow to cool. This is a great recipe to do the night before and leave in the oven.

To make the filling, whip the plant cream, maple syrup, vanilla, and lime zest and juice in a bowl until stiff peaks form.

To assemble the pavlova, spoon the cream into the trough you made in the ring and then arrange the fruits and herbs on top. Serve immediately.

INGREDIENTS

FOR THE WREATH:

250 ml (8½ fl oz/1 cup) aquafaba (liquid from tinned chickpeas)
280 g (10 oz/1¼ cups) caster (superfine) sugar, sifted
1 teaspoon cornflour (cornstarch)
⅓ teaspoon cream of tartar

FOR THE FILLING:

260 ml (9 fl oz/generous 1 cup) whippable plant cream
1 tablespoon maple syrup
1 vanilla pod (bean), split and the seeds scraped out, or 1 teaspoon vanilla paste or extract
zest and juice of 1 lime
500 g (1 lb 2 oz) seasonal fruits (such as citruses, strawberries, raspberries and blueberries)
a few mint and basil leaves, to decorate

MOVEABLE FEASTS

I love a picnic!
Fun, adventure, fresh
air, yummy food, family,
friends, enjoying nature.
If, like me, you love nature,
are a gourmand and enjoy
food you have prepared
by yourself, then this
movable feast is a perfect
solution for you. Relax, get
away from everyday life,
discover nature and enjoy
an outdoor feast.

CORONATION JACK SANDWICH

This is my take on the classic coronation chicken sandwich. I am using jackfruit here, which has a great stringy texture, along with creamy mayonnaise and other ingredients that make up this classic. The sandwich includes healthy greens and crisps for extra oomph!

MAKES
2 SANDWICHES

INGREDIENTS

400 g (14 oz) tin of jackfruit,
  drained and rinsed
1 tablespoon olive oil
2 spring onions (scallions),
  finely sliced
1 small apple, finely diced
200 g (7 oz/¾ cup) plant mayonnaise
1 tablespoon curry powder
1 tablespoon currants or raisins,
  chopped
juice of ½ lemon
salt and pepper, to taste

TO SERVE:

sourdough or baguette

OPTIONAL EXTRAS:

handful of coriander
  (cilantro) leaves
handful of cress or watercress
crisps (I love a truffle crisp)

METHOD

Preheat the oven to 200°C (400°F/gas 6). Line a baking tray (pan) with baking parchment.

Shred the jackfruit or, if it is in chunks, cut into thin strips or smaller pieces. Spread the jackfruit out on the lined tray, drizzle with the olive oil and season with salt and pepper.

Cook the jackfruit in the oven for 20–30 minutes until stringy and crispy – it will look like shredded chicken. Remove and set aside to cool.

Once the jackfruit is cooled, add the remainder of the ingredients to the tray and mix together well.

Use the Coronation Jack to fill a sourdough or baguette sandwich, adding your choice of extras such as coriander, cress or watercress and crisps (or all of these) if required.

COOK'S TIP:

I recommend using proper sandwich bread, watercress and truffle crisps for the most epic of sandwiches!

UPSIDE-DOWN
LEEK SAVOURY BREAD

/

I love leeks and this is such an amazing way to show them off. The leeks are sweet and the batter is spongy, and this is an excellent dish to bring along for a picnic.

SERVES
6–8

INGREDIENTS

4 large leeks, washed thoroughly
   between the layers
2–3 tablespoons olive oil
1 tablespoon maple syrup
pinch of salt and pepper

FOR THE BATTER:

100 g (3½ oz/1 cup) chickpea
   (gram) flour
40 g (1½ oz/⅓ cup) buckwheat flour
½ teaspoon bicarbonate of soda
   (baking soda)
1 teaspoon baking powder
pinch of curry powder
pinch of salt and pepper
360 ml (12 fl oz/1½ cups) water
1 tablespoon apple cider vinegar
10 g (½ oz) chives, snipped

METHOD

Preheat the oven to 180°C (350°F/gas 4). Line a 21 cm (8¼ in) round baking tin (pan) with baking parchment.

Slice the leeks into 1.5–2 cm (½–¾ in) rounds, stopping at the dark green part.

Add 1–2 tablespoons of the olive oil to a large frying pan (skillet), arrange the leek, rounds standing up, in one layer across the bottom and fry for 5 minutes until nice and browned on the bottom (don't turn the leek rounds over).

While the leeks are frying, whisk all the batter ingredients together in a bowl. Set aside.

Mix 1 tablespoon of the olive oil, the maple syrup, and salt and pepper together in a bowl. Pour into the lined baking tray and spread across the base.

Place the caramelised leeks in one layer in the tray, browned side facing down, and cook in the oven for 20 minutes.

Remove the leeks from the oven, pour the batter mixture evenly over the leeks and cook for a further 15 minutes.

Remove from the oven and leave to cool for 10–15 minutes, then turn upside down onto your serving dish.

COOK'S TIP:

You can save the green part of the leek to use in another dish, such as a stir-fry, soup or curry.

POTATO SALAD WITH DILL,
CRISPY ONIONS & CAVIAR
—PAGE 90—

ICED GINGER &
TURMERIC LEMONADE
—PAGE 103—

CHILLED GREEN
AJO BLANCO
—PAGE 91—

POTATO SALAD WITH DILL, CRISPY ONIONS & CAVIAR

/

My Scandinavian roots are popping up again here. We love a good creamy potato salad. This one features caramelised onions, both ladled through it and on top. Creamy, satisfying and good-looking. What's not to like?

SERVES
6–8

O

METHOD

Cook the new potatoes in a saucepan of boiling water for 15–20 minutes until soft.

While the potatoes are cooking, fry the onion in the olive oil in a frying pan (skillet) until browned and crispy. Set aside to cool and remove a small amount as garnish.

Drain the potatoes and return to the pan. If some are larger, cut them in half. Add the fried onions, peas (except for the peas in their pods/sugar snap peas), mayonnaise, yoghurt, chives, dill, mustard and salt and pepper, and mix together well.

Serve on a platter or in a large bowl, topped with the crispy onion you set aside, some chopped dill and the freshly blanched peas in their pod/sugar snap peas. Top with seaweed caviar.

INGREDIENTS

1 kg (2 lb 4 oz) baby new potatoes
1 large onion (about 350 g/12 oz), sliced into half-moons
2 tablespoons olive oil
150 g (5 oz) frozen peas, defrosted
100 g (3½ oz) peas in their pods or sugar snap peas, blanched, for topping
150 g (5 oz/⅔ cup) plant mayonnaise
50 g (2 oz/¼ cup) plant yoghurt
30 g (1 oz) chives, snipped
30 g (1 oz) dill fronds, chopped, plus extra to garnish
1 tablespoon Dijon mustard
1 jar of seaweed caviar (optional)
salt and pepper, to taste

CHILLED GREEN AJO BLANCO

/

A refreshing drink/cold soup that can be carried in a flask and enjoyed with an accompanying sandwich or as a side dish. It contains lots of goodness with a hint of garlic for freshness and an extra kick.

INGREDIENTS

240 g (8½ oz) blanched almonds
90 g (3 oz) stale bread
500 ml (17 fl oz/2 cups) unsweetened
    plant milk (I like oat milk)
1 cucumber, peeled and sliced
150 ml (5 fl oz/scant ⅔ cup) olive oil
1 handful of spinach or watercress
2 tablespoons apple cider vinegar
1 garlic clove
juice of 1 lemon
salt and pepper, to taste

TO SERVE:

a few green grapes, sliced
olive oil, for drizzling

METHOD

Place all the ingredients in a food processor or blender and blitz until smooth.

Chill in the fridge until you're ready to eat.

COOK'S TIP:

Traditionally, if not being taken on a picnic, this chilled soup is served with an extra drizzle of olive oil and topped with finely sliced grapes.

ROASTED SWEET POTATO & BUTTER BEAN SALAD

A movable feast that ticks all the boxes: protein, carbs, greens, flavour and comfort. It's a dish that's feel-good for both you and the planet.

INGREDIENTS

2 medium sweet potatoes, peeled and cut into medium-size chunks
2 tablespoons olive oil
pinch of salt
480 g (1 lb 1 oz) tinned or jarred butter (lima) beans, drained and rinsed
1 shallot, sliced
2 handfuls of salad greens, such as rocket (arugula) and watercress
30 g (1 oz) parsley leaves, chopped
30 g (1 oz) basil leaves, chopped

FOR THE DRESSING:

2 tablespoons olive oil
2 tablespoons apple cider vinegar
1 tablespoon maple syrup or honey
1 teaspoon miso paste
1 teaspoon Dijon mustard
2–3 pinches of salt and pepper

TO SERVE:

handful of toasted walnuts

METHOD

Preheat the oven to 200°C (400°F/gas 6). Line a medium baking tray (pan) with baking parchment.

Spread the chunks of sweet potato over the base of the baking tray, drizzle with the olive oil and season with salt. Roast in the oven for 30 minutes, then turn the potato over and return to the oven for a further 30 minutes, or until crisp and golden. Set aside to cool.

Mix all the ingredients for the dressing together in a large bowl, then add the butter beans, shallot and roasted sweet potatoes.

Chop the salad greens and add to the bowl along with the parsley and basil.

Just before serving, mix well and serve with toasted walnuts sprinkled over the top.

COOK'S TIP:

If you are making the salad in advance, don't mix the ingredients in the big bowl until the last minute. This way, the greens won't spoil and will be freshly dressed. If you are making the salad for a picnic, layer the ingredients in a large, lidded container instead of a bowl, and shake upside down before serving.

KIMBAP

/

Kimbap is a Korean dish made from sheets of dried seaweed filled with cooked rice (seasoned with sesame oil and salt) and a variety of fillings, which are then rolled up tightly and served in bite-size slices. It is very similar to Japanese sushi but there are two differences: the rice and the filling. The rice in kimbap is seasoned with sesame oil and a bit of salt, while for sushi it is flavoured with vinegar. Japanese sushi rolls are usually filled with fish and/or vegetables, whereas kimbap is filled with cooked proteins such as bulgogi and also vegetables. I have had kimbap on many occasions during trips to South Korea. It is a great dish that can be easily transported.

O

METHOD

Rinse the sushi rice thoroughly, then cook according to the directions on the packet.

While the rice is cooking you can prepare the fillings. Choose a variety of fillings from the Ingredients list. Slice any fresh ingredients lengthways into thin strips.

If you are using cooked fillings, choose a few and cook each one separately with some sesame oil and a dash of tamari/soy sauce for saltiness. If you are cooking tofu or tempeh, coat in some cornflour beforehand and fry in oil, adding some tamari/soy sauce for saltiness, then slice into strips when cooled down.

The beauty of kimbap is that you can add a lot more fillings than you can with sushi. It is all about using generous quantities of filling and mixing raw/cooked and fermented ingredients with a dollop of something wet and creamy like mayonnaise or hummus.

When the rice has cooled down, add a small drizzle of sesame seed oil – just a tad as this is also one of the differences between Japanese sushi rolls and Korean kimbap.

INGREDIENTS

150 g (5 oz/¾ cup) sushi rice
1 packet of nori sheets
    (you'll need 4–6 sheets)
sesame oil

COOKED FILLINGS:

selection of sliced vegetables
    (such as spinach leaves,
    onions, mushrooms, asparagus
    and baby corn)
tofu (I prefer organic)
smoked tofu
tempeh
cornflour (cornstarch), for frying
    the tofu and tempeh
1 tablespoon tamari or soy sauce
dash of olive oil

FRESH FILLINGS:

carrots
avocado
cucumber
asparagus
spring onions (scallions)

FERMENTED FILLINGS:

kimchi
pickled daikon
pickled ginger
burdock root

WET FILLINGS:

mayonnaise
hummus
wasabi
sesame oil

Once you have all the other ingredients ready, it's time to roll everything up! The easiest way to roll kimbap is with a bamboo sushi mat, but this is not essential as you can also use a dish towel. Keep a bowl of water to hand beside your workstation.

To make the dipping sauce, mix all the ingredients together in a small bowl and set aside until ready to serve.

To assemble, place a sheet of nori on a clean plate, with the shiny side facing down and the long side running vertically. Dip your fingers in the bowl and add a thin layer of rice on top of the seaweed. Press the rice down with your fingers to cover the seaweed evenly, leaving 2–3 cm [¾–1¼ in] clear at the top.

Layer your choice of filling ingredients horizontally. You don't want to over- or under-fill the kimbap, so use the first roll as a 'tester' to see how much you can fit in [this will depend on how large you sliced the vegetables].

Once the filling is in place, lift up the bottom edge and roll over the filling ingredients. Press firmly against the bamboo mat or dish towel and keep going until you reach the top. The seaweed should hold together at the end due to the moisture in the rice.

Brush the roll lightly with some sesame oil. Using a sharp knife, cut the roll into eight equal pieces. In some places in South Korea the slices are not cut all the way through and are wrapped in some brown paper [almost like a burrito], so you can tear off pieces on the go and the rice doesn't dry out as quickly.

Wipe your knife with a damp cloth or paper towel after every cut to ensure you make clean cuts. And there you have it! A simple and easy kimbap recipe.

COOK'S TIP

Sliced kimbap can be refrigerated in an airtight container for several hours without compromising the flavour and the texture. However, if you store the kimbap overnight, the rice will most likely dry out. If you want to eat the kimbap next day, simply leave the rolls unsliced and keep well packaged in the fridge.

MAKES 4–6 ROLLS
[READY FOR
CUTTING]

DIPPING SAUCE

5 tablespoons tamari
    or strong soy sauce
1 teaspoon gojujang
1 tablespoon maple syrup
½ grated garlic clove
½ grated piece of ginger root
1 tablespoon sesame oil

ROLY POLY CAKE

Who doesn't love a roly poly cake? Filled with cream, jam and berries, this one's made extra special with a few adjustments and some spice for added colour and flair. Adored by little ones and big ones alike.

SERVES 6

METHOD

Preheat the oven to 180°C (350°C/gas 4). Line a large baking tray (pan) with baking parchment.

To make the cake, cream the butter and sugar together in a large bowl until soft and fluffy.

In another bowl, whisk the aquafaba until it is white, fluffy and soft peaks have formed. This will take a good 10 minutes. Set aside.

Add the flour, turmeric, baking powder, vinegar, vanilla, plant milk, and salt to the creamed butter and sugar. Mix to incorporate.

Gently fold the aquafaba through the mix then spread it over the base of the tray. Bake for 12–15 minutes.

Check if the cake is ready by inserting a skewer into the middle and seeing if it comes out clean (it may need a few more minutes). Remove the cake from the oven and place on a wire rack to cool completely.

Meanwhile, to make the filling, whisk the coconut cream in a bowl and add the remaining ingredients (except for the jam). Keep the filling cool.

Once the cake has cooled down completely, remove from the baking tray and spread with a generous layer of cherry jam followed by the cream filling.

Roll the cake into a tight roll, starting with the longer side until it forms a beautiful roly poly cake. Keep refrigerated until you're ready to serve.

Just before serving, top with whipped cream and a cherry to make it extra pretty.

INGREDIENTS

FOR THE CAKE:

120 g (4¼ oz) vegan butter, plus extra for greasing
160 g (5¾ oz/⅔ cup) caster (superfine) sugar (caster sugar keeps the cake light and airy)
3 tablespoons aquafaba (liquid from tinned chickpeas)
300 ml (7 fl oz/scant 1 cup) plant milk (I like oat milk)
320 g (11¼ oz/2½ cups) self-raising flour
2 teaspoons baking powder
1 tablespoon apple cider vinegar
1 teaspoon ground turmeric
1 vanilla pod (bean), split and the seeds scraped out, or 1 teaspoon vanilla paste or extract
pinch of salt

FOR THE FILLING:

160 ml (5½ fl oz/⅔ cup) coconut cream or refrigerated full-fat tinned coconut milk (see *Cook's Tips* on page 148)
1 vanilla pod (bean), split and the seeds scraped out, or 1 teaspoon vanilla paste or extract
1 tablespoon maple syrup
zest of ½ orange
1 jar of cherry jam (about 340 g/12 oz)

FOR THE TOPPING:

200 ml (7 fl oz/scant 1 cup) whippable plant cream
fresh cherries, pitted and cut in half

CREAMY LAYERED TRIFLE IN A JAR

I love custard, I love berries, I love summer … and this dish screams all of these things. It is happiness in a jar! The best thing about it is that you can take it with you on an adventure and share it with someone you love.

METHOD

First, make the sponge and custard then allow to cool.

To make the cream for the trifle, gently combine all the ingredients together in a bowl and set aside.

For the fruit layer, mix the balsamic vinegar, sugar, basil and vanilla together in a bowl, then add the fruit and toss until are well coated. Leave to marinate while you make the cake base and allow to cool completely.

To assemble the trifle, use one large pretty bowl or six individual glass jars (perfect for on the move). Create the trifle by starting with a sponge base, then add a layer of custard and a layer of fruit. To finish, top with the whipped cream and basil leaves.

COOK'S TIP:

If you would like to make *Whipped Coconut Cream* from coconut milk, see page 187.

INGREDIENTS

FOR THE SPONGE:

1 *Vanilla Sponge Cake Base* (see page 184), baked in a 31 x 37 cm (12 x 14 in) baking tray (pan) as a sheet cake

FOR THE CUSTARD:

1 batch of *Homemade Custard* (see page 182).

FOR THE CREAM:

160 ml (5½ fl oz/⅔ cup) coconut cream, whipped (see *Cook's Tip*)
zest of 1 lime
½ vanilla pod (bean), split and the seeds scraped out, or ½ teaspoon vanilla paste or extract
2 tablespoons maple syrup

FOR THE FRUIT LAYER:

2 tablespoons balsamic vinegar
1 tablespoon caster (superfine) sugar
a few sprigs of basil (leaves only), chopped, plus extra to decorate
½ vanilla pod (bean), split and the seeds scraped out, or ½ teaspoon vanilla paste or extract
500 g/1 lb 2 oz) mix of strawberries de-stemmed and quartered, and raspberries

ICED GINGER & TURMERIC LEMONADE

A take on lemonade that includes some of my favourite ingredients. I have spent a lot of time in Bali and have incorporated my favourites here for a refreshing yet zingy drink!

MAKES 1 LITRE
(34 FL OZ/4 CUPS)

INGREDIENTS

1 litre (34 fl oz/4 cups)
    coconut water
a thumbnail-size piece
    of turmeric root
3 cm (1¼ in) piece of ginger root
pinch of black pepper
3 tablespoons honey or maple syrup
zest and juice of 1 orange
zest and juice of 1 lemon

METHOD

Place all the ingredients in a food processor or blender and blitz until smooth. You don't need to peel the ginger or turmeric roots, just wash them well.

Once blended, strain through a sieve and add the lemonade to a glass bottle(s).

COOK'S TIPS:

- Once the lemonade has been strained, you can keep the remaining pulp and add it to smoothies.

- If you are going on a picnic, put the bottle of lemonade in the freezer beforehand and use it as an ice pack to keep the rest of your picnic cool.

- If keeping the lemonade for any length of time, it's advisable to sterilise the bottle(s) and sieve first.

- Wash the blender in cold water straight away to get rid of the stains.

HALLOWEEN AND
THANKSGIVING

The recipes in this chapter are a nod to the Americans and their two key holidays – Halloween and Thanksgiving – which seem to be getting adopted elsewhere. Especially Halloween. These dishes are a great way of celebrating autumnal produce and gearing up for the colder months ahead. I particularly like the pumpkin dishes.

BLINIS WITH HERBED ALMOND FETA & FIGS

A great starter that is simple to prepare. You can make the batter for the blinis and the almond feta ahead, and then simply put everything together when your guests arrive.

Note: The Almond Feta base (see page 182) should be made the day before because it needs to sit in the fridge overnight.

MAKES
30–40 BLINIS

METHOD

Mix all the ingredients for the blinis together (except the olive oil) in a bowl until well combined.

Heat some olive oil in a frying pan (skillet), then drop spoonfuls of the blini mixture into the pan to make little, round, bite-size pancakes and cook on both sides until golden brown.

Whip all the ingredients for the herbed almond feta in a bowl until nice and fluffy.

To assemble, put the blinis on a serving platter and dollop some whipped almond feta on top of each one. Finish with some sliced figs and a drizzle of balsamic vinegar and sprinkle with herbs.

COOK'S TIP:

You can make the blinis and almond feta in advance, then put the dish together just before your guests arrive.

INGREDIENTS

FOR THE BLINIS:

120 g (4 oz/1 cup) buckwheat flour
90 g (3½ oz/¾ cup) plain (all-purpose) flour (for a gluten-free version, use 70 g/2½ oz/½ cup rice flour)
220 ml (7 fl oz/scant 1 cup) plant milk (I like oat milk)
1 teaspoon apple cider vinegar
½ teaspoon bicarbonate of soda (baking soda)
½ teaspoon baking soda
salt and pepper, to taste
olive oil, for frying

FOR THE HERBED ALMOND FETA:

Almond Feta (see page 182)
½ garlic clove
zest and juice of 1 lemon
dill frond, chopped
salt and pepper, to taste

TO SERVE:

whole figs, sliced
balsamic vinegar
micro herbs
thyme sprigs

WHOLE ROASTED STUFFED MARROW

SERVES 4–6,
DEPENDING ON
THE SIZE OF
YOUR MARROW

The marrow is such an underestimated vegetable and not used or praised enough. It can be daunting because of its size and mysterious spongy texture. Cooking it low and slow is the key here! This turned out to be one of everyone's favourite dishes when we were testing the recipes for the book – as I'm sure you will all agree!

INGREDIENTS

1 large marrow (if you can't find marrow use 2 large white courgettes/zucchinis)
½ red onion, finely chopped
2 tablespoons olive oil
75 g (2½ oz) almonds, blitzed
1 tablespoon barbecue spice
½ teaspoon chilli (hot pepper) flakes
salt and pepper, to taste
dill fronds, to garnish

METHOD

If you are barbecuing the marrow, prepare and heat up the barbecue in advance or, alternatively, preheat the oven to 200°C (400°F/gas 6).

Prepare the marrow by slicing it in half and scooping out the insides with a spoon, then set aside the two halves. Chop the scooped insides into small pieces (about 2 cm/¾ in) and add to a bowl.

Add the onion, olive oil, blitzed almonds and spices to the bowl of chopped marrow and mix well. Start adding the mixture to one half of the scooped-out marrow shell. Once the marrow is filled, place the other half on top to close and shut the marrow. Seal the marrow securely with string (making sure you use a double knot) or wrap tightly in aluminium foil if you are barbecuing it.

Place the marrow in a large baking tray (pan) lined with baking parchment and cook in the oven for 45 minutes to 1 hour. Alternatively, pop in a lidded barbecue for a good 45 minutes. If you're going for the barbecue option, make sure this is sealed properly!

Once the marrow is cooked, it will be nice and soft, and easily sliced into lovely pieces to be eaten as a side dish or as it is.

CREAMY SWEET POTATO & LEEK BAKE

I adore potatoes! You may also have noticed that I love leeks, too. The combination of two varieties of potatoes, leeks and cream, all slow cooked in an oven dish, is my dream come true.

INGREDIENTS

600 g (1 lb 5 oz) sweet potatoes, peeled and washed
600 g (1 lb 5 oz) floury baking potatoes, peeled and washed
1 leek (green part and all)
750 ml (25 fl oz/3 cups) plant cream (I like oat cream)
1 tablespoon Dijon mustard
a sprig of thyme (leaves only)
1 tablespoon vegan butter
1–2 garlic cloves
salt and pepper, to taste

METHOD

Preheat the oven to 180°C (350°F/gas 4).

Slice the potatoes in half using a mandoline (if you have one); otherwise slice them very thinly.

Chop off the end of the leek, slice in half lengthways and wash well between the layers. Then chop into 1 cm (½ in) chunks, including the green part.

Add the cream, mustard, thyme leaves, and salt and pepper to a bowl and mix well. Set aside.

Grease the inside of a shallow rectangular oven dish with the butter. Grate the garlic into the dish, spreading it around evenly and mixing into the butter. This will give a lovely garlicky hint to the whole dish.

Using half of the potatoes, fill the base of the dish with layers of both types of potatoes, then add a middle layer of all the leeks and use the remaining potatoes to form the top layer. Make sure you push the top layer down well as the leeks may be a bit springy.

Pour the cream mixture evenly over the top, making sure everything is covered well.

Pop into the oven for 1 hour until lovely and crispy on top.

COOK'S TIP:

Use larger potatoes rather than smaller ones so you spend less time peeling.

ROASTED CAULIFLOWER
& FENNEL ON PEA SMASH
—PAGE 115—

TARRAGON & MAPLE-GLAZED CARROTS ON CHESTNUT MASH

Tarragon is so under-appreciated that I'd like to use this recipe as an opportunity to highlight this gem of a herb. Combined here with the sweetness of carrots and maple syrup on chestnut mash, it is a real winner.

SERVES
4

INGREDIENTS

4–6 carrots, in a variety of colours
3–4 tablespoons olive oil
1 teaspoon maple syrup
1 teaspoon Dijon mustard
10 g (½ oz) tarragon leaves, torn

FOR THE CHESTNUT MASH:

400 g (14 oz) chestnuts
    vacuum-packed)
250 ml (8½ fl oz/1 cup) plant milk
    (I like oat milk)
280 g (10 oz) butter (lima) beans,
    drained and rinsed
300 ml (10 fl oz/1¼ cups)
    plant cream
1 tablespoon miso paste
salt and pepper, to taste

SUGGESTED TOPPINGS:

olive oil
maple syrup
tarragon leaves
pomegranate seeds

METHOD

Preheat the oven to 200°C (400°F/gas 6).

Wash, peel and halve the carrots lengthways. Place on a baking tray (pan) lined with baking parchment.

Make a marinade by mixing the olive oil, maple syrup and Dijon mustard in a small bowl.

Baste the carrots all over with the marinade, sprinkle over the tarragon and cook in the oven for 30 minutes, or until nice and golden brown.

While the carrots are cooking, make the chestnut mash. Add the chestnuts to a saucepan with the plant milk and heat through for 5–10 minutes. Add the chestnuts and milk to a food processor or blender along with the butter beans, cream and miso paste, then whizz until you have a smooth mash. Season to taste.

Once the carrots are cooked, create a smooth bed of chestnut mash on a serving plate and arrange the carrots on top. If you wish, drizzle with olive oil and maple syrup, then sprinkle over some tarragon leaves and pomegranate seeds.

ROASTED CAULIFLOWER & FENNEL ON PEA SMASH

When you roast cauliflower and fennel slowly, they become sticky and sweet. And it's this that makes them taste so delicious.

Note: If you are using Almond Feta (see page 182) as a topping, this should be made the day before because it needs to sit in the fridge overnight.

SERVES
4

METHOD

Preheat the oven to 200°C (400°F/gas 6). Line a large oven dish or baking tray (pan) with baking parchment.

Slice the cauliflower head and fennel bulb vertically into 'steaks' (about 2 cm/¾ in deep) through the core. If you wish, you can cut the cauliflower into florets instead.

Spread the cauliflower, fennel, olive oil, paprika, and salt and pepper over the base of the dish/tray. Sprinkle with the nigella seeds and roast in the oven for 30–40 minutes until golden brown.

While the vegetables are roasting, make the pea smash. Add the frozen peas to a saucepan filled with the plant cream and heat through gently.

Once the cream has warmed and the peas thawed, remove from the heat (be careful not to overcook), and add to a food processor or blender with the garlic and mint. Blitz until everything is fully combined.

When the vegetables are ready, spread the pea smash over a serving platter and arrange the cauliflower and fennel on top. If you wish, finish with generous dollops of almond feta, toasted nuts and sprigs of mint.

INGREDIENTS

1 cauliflower head
    (leaves and all)
1 fennel bulb
2 tablespoons olive oil
1 teaspoon paprika powder
1 teaspoon nigella seeds
salt and pepper, to taste

FOR THE PEA SMASH:

500 g (1 lb 2 oz) frozen peas
200 ml (7 fl oz/scant 1 cup)
    plant cream (I like oat cream)
1 garlic clove
30 g (1 oz) mint leaves

SUGGESTED TOPPINGS:

Almond Feta (see page 182)
toasted nuts
sprigs of mint

SAVOURY PUMPKIN FOCACCIA WITH PESTO

⟲ ❋

I wanted to find a way to make good use of all the Halloween pumpkin we tend to buy and only use for decoration. This bread looks stunning with the sliced pumpkin on top for decoration.

SERVES
4–6

METHOD

Add the water, yeast, sugar and salt to a bowl and stir well until everything is dissolved. (Make sure the water is lukewarm and not boiling hot.)

Once dissolved, add the flour and combine well with a spoon or dough whisk to form a nice dough. Scrape any excess dough from the sides of the bowl, then add some olive oil to the sides (to prevent the focaccia sticking when it rises).

Cover the bowl loosely (I like to use a shower cap or dish towel) and leave somewhere warm to rise for 3–4 hours, or overnight in the fridge. You can make this in the morning to eat in the evening or make in the evening and leave in the fridge overnight for the next day.

When the dough has doubled in size and is slightly bubbly, it is ready for the next step.

Preheat the oven to 220°C (430°F/gas 8). Cover the bottom of a non-stick baking tray (pan) – or one lined with baking parchment – generously with 2 tablespoons olive oil, then tip the focaccia dough onto the tray. Spread out evenly with your fingers, poking small dents into the dough with your fingertips. You can use some more olive oil here if necessary, to make this easier.

Next arrange the sliced pumpkin and onion on top of the dough, along with the thyme sprigs, pushing everything down gently so it bakes nicely into the focaccia.

INGREDIENTS

500 ml (17 fl oz/2 cups)
    lukewarm water
1 x 7 g (1¼ oz) sachet
    of fast-action dried yeast
1 tablespoon sugar
pinch of salt
600 g (1 lb 5 oz) plain
    (all-purpose) flour
2 tablespoons olive oil,
    plus extra for drizzling

FOR THE TOPPING:

1 small squash or pumpkin,
    very thinly sliced
1 yellow onion, very thinly sliced
handful of thyme sprigs
salt and pepper, to taste

FOR THE ROCKET PESTO:

60 g (2 oz) rocket (arugula),
    plus extra to serve (optional)
60 g (2 oz) pumpkin seeds
60 ml (2 fl oz/¼ cup) olive oil
zest and juice of 1 lemon
salt and pepper, to taste

Sprinkle some salt and pepper on top and bake in the oven for 30 minutes until golden brown.

While the focaccia is baking, make the pesto by blitzing all the ingredients in a food processor or blender. Once combined set aside.

When the focaccia is ready, leave on a wire cooling rack for 10 minutes. Once cooled, drizzle the pesto on top and serve warm. Sprinkle with extra rocket, if you like.

BROWN SUGAR
SPICED APPLE CAKE

This is hands down my favourite
cake recipe. The apples, the brown
sugar and the caramelisation of
both is a match made in heaven.
This is also happens to be gluten free!

SERVES
6–8

METHOD

Preheat the oven to 180°C (350°F/gas 4). Line a 20 cm (8 in)
cake pan with baking parchment or use a good-quality
silicone mould.

Add all the cake ingredients to a food processor and blitz
for about 5 minutes until everything is well incorporated.
Pour the mixture into the cake pan.

For the topping, mix the sugar and cinnamon together
in a small bowl, then sprinkle a layer of the mixture over
the cake. Arrange the apples neatly to cover the top of the
cake, then sprinkle the remaining sugar and cinnamon over
the apples.

Bake in the middle of the oven for 45 minutes. Switch the
oven off and leave the cake to sit in the oven for a further
15 minutes.

Remove the cake from the oven, then transfer to a wire
rack to cool. Once cooled pop the cake out of the pan
onto a serving plate.

I love this cake served with a good helping of vanilla
custard.

INGREDIENTS

FOR THE CAKE:

200 g (7 oz/2 cups) almond flour
3 tablespoons buckwheat flour
250 ml (8½ fl oz/1 cup) plant milk
125 ml (4 fl oz/½ cup) maple syrup
125 ml (4 fl oz/½ cup) melted
    coconut oil
1 teaspoon baking powder
½ teaspoon bicarbonate of soda
    (baking soda)
1 vanilla pod (bean), split and the
    seeds scraped out, or 1 teaspoon
    vanilla paste or extract
pinch of pink Himalayan salt

FOR THE TOPPING:

2 tablespoons soft brown sugar
2 teaspoons ground cinnamon
4 apples, unpeeled and cored,
    then quartered and sliced
    into thin half-moons

TO SERVE:

plant-based vanilla custard
    (see *Homemade Custard*,
    page 183, to make your own)

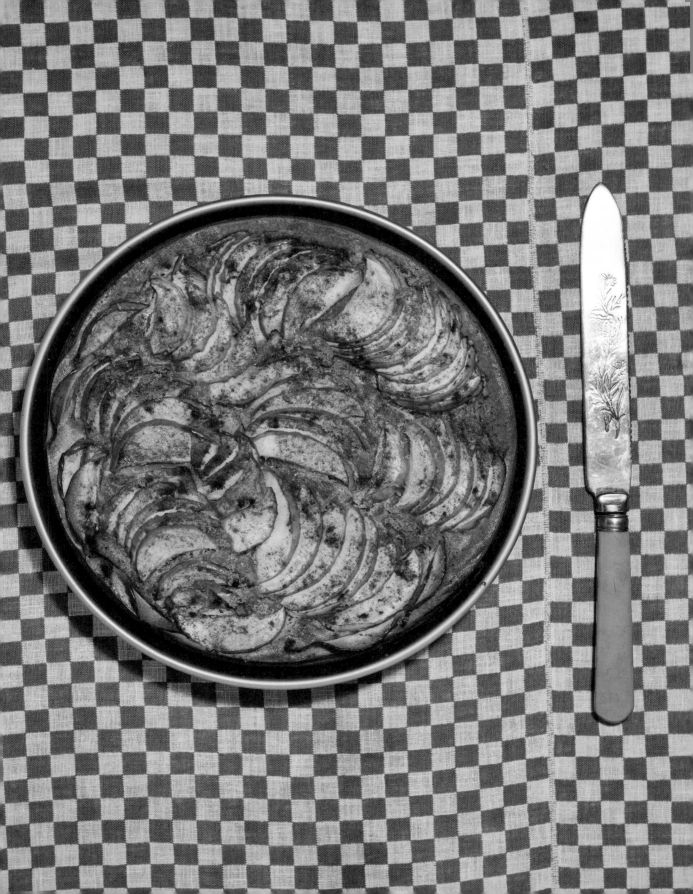

CINNAMON CARAMEL TOFFEE APPLES

A homage to my childhood but made slightly better for you. This is a great recipe to make with your children – it will look good and taste even better.

MAKES
12

METHOD

Line a plate or tray (that will fit in the fridge) with greaseproof (waxed) paper.

To make the caramel, warm the coconut milk and sugar in a saucepan over a medium heat.

Add the vanilla, cinnamon and salt to the pan, bring to the boil, then reduce to a simmer for 40 minutes until the caramel has thickened and turned caramel brown. Stir occasionally to make sure the caramel doesn't burn. A great way of knowing if the caramel is ready is to see if it sticks to the back of a spoon.

Prepare the toppings by chopping them into small pieces and putting each one in a separate bowl.

Insert a popsicle stick into each of the apples.

Once the caramel sauce is ready, dip the apples in the sauce, making sure you coat as much of the surface as possible, then dip them in your favourite toppings.

Sit the coated apples on the lined plate/tray, with the stick facing up, and keep in the fridge for at least 2 hours, or until the caramel hardens.

INGREDIENTS

12 (very) small apples
12 wooden popsicle sticks

FOR THE CINNAMON CARAMEL:

400 g (14 oz) tin of full-fat coconut milk
280 g (10 oz/1½ cups) brown or coconut sugar
½ vanilla pod (bean), split and the seeds scraped out, or ½ teaspoon vanilla paste or extract
1 teaspoon ground cinnamon
pinch of salt

SUGGESTED TOPPINGS:

pistachios
pumpkin seeds
hemp hearts
sesame seeds
hazelnuts
dried flower petals

SPICED
PUMPKIN PIE

/

I couldn't leave the pumpkin pie out, could I? This lovely pie includes a pinch of spice and has lots of creamy texture. It goes well with ice cream or some whipped cream! It's a must in my humble opinion.

↻ ❄

SERVES
6–8

○

METHOD

Preheat the oven to 180°C (350°F/gas 4). Grease a cake or pie pan (with a removable base so the pie will come out easily) with some butter.

Make the pastry by adding all the dry ingredients to a bowl. Use your hands to rub the chopped butter into the flour mix. Then add the milk little by little and mix well to form a dough. You can either use the pastry straightaway or, if you have time, rest it somewhere warm for 15–20 minutes. Alternatively, keep in the fridge overnight.

Roll the pastry dough into a disc that's larger than the base of the cake/pie pan, with enough to go up the sides. Put the pastry in the pan and use your index fingers and thumbs to press into the base and sides so it lines the whole pan. Trim off any excess dough that comes over the edges with a knife. You can use the excess dough to create a criss cross pattern on top of the pie if you like.

Prick the base of the pastry with a fork and pre-cook in the oven for 10 minutes.

Meanwhile, add all the ingredients for the filling to a food processor or blender and blitz until well combined.

When the pie case is ready, remove from the oven and add the pumpkin filling. Smooth the filling flat with a palette knife and add a criss-cross pattern if using, then bake in the oven for 45 minutes.

While the pie is baking, whip the cream with the maple syrup and vanilla. Chill in the fridge until you are ready to serve.

INGREDIENTS

FOR THE PASTRY:

250 g (9 oz/2 cups) plain (all-purpose) flour
pinch of salt
pinch of sugar
115 g (4 oz) vegan butter, chopped into small pieces, plus extra for greasing
60 ml (2 fl oz/¼ cup) plant milk (I like oat milk)

FOR THE FILLING:

480 g (1 lb 1 oz) pumpkin purée (see Cook's Tips)
120 g (4 oz/1¼ cups) ground almonds (almond meal)
100 g (3½ oz/½ cup) brown or coconut sugar
100 ml (3½ fl oz/scant ½ cup) plant milk
60 g (2 oz) vegan butter
60 g (2 oz/½ cup) plain (all-purpose) flour
2 cm (¾ in) piece of ginger root, peeled and grated
1 teaspoon ground cinnamon
1 teaspoon ground cardamom
½ teaspoon ground cloves
½ teaspoon baking powder

TO SERVE:

280 ml (10 fl oz/1¼ cups) whippable plant cream
1 tablespoon maple syrup
1 vanilla pod (bean), split and the seeds scraped out, or 1 teaspoon vanilla paste or extract

Once the pie is ready, remove from the oven and allow to cool completely before serving with the whipped cream.

COOK'S TIP:

An easy way to cook a whole pumpkin, skin and all, is to roast it in the oven at 180°C (350°F/gas 4) for 1 hour. Once cooked, simply cut off the top, remove the seeds and use the cooked pumpkin for this and other recipes, such as risottos and salads. The pumpkin will last a week in the fridge and you can dip into it whenever you need it!

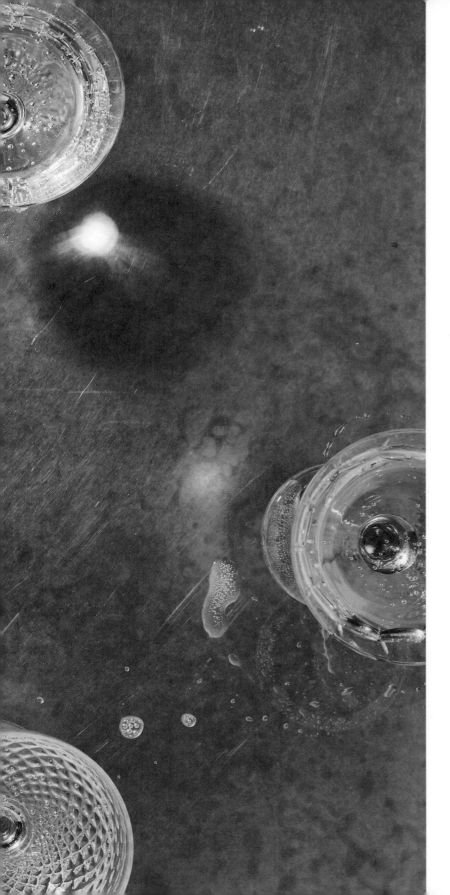

CHRISTMAS AND NEW YEAR

I cherish Christmas. It is the month of celebrations. I love everything about the season, from opening up advent calendars to putting up decorations. Seeing friends and family socially to spend hours on cooking because, well, it is Christmas and definitely worth celebrating! Coming from a multicultural background I always celebrated Scandinavian (Norwegian) Christmas on the 24th and Bulgarian/Danish Christmas on the 25th. Today we still celebrate the Scandinavian version and the UK version from my husband's side of the family with elements of Bulgarian and Danish from my childhood.

LENTIL PÂTÉ WITH CARAMELISED PEARS

This is a great pâté that can be made in individual pots or as a terrine. The thyme and pear offer an extra layer of flavour. This is one of those dishes that gets better with time.

SERVES
4–6

METHOD

Start by cooking the lentils, ensuring they are nice and soft. Once cooked, drain thoroughly and set aside to cool.

Fry the onion and garlic in some olive oil in a saucepan for a few minutes until soft.

Roughly chop or tear the mushrooms, including the stems, then add to the pan and cook for a further 5–10 minutes. Add the lentils and give everything a good stir.

Add the maple syrup, tamari/soy sauce, sherry, thyme, and salt and pepper. Stir well for a couple of minutes.

Transfer the mixture to a food processor or blender with the olive oil and blitz until smooth.

Pour into your desired pâté pot – for example, one large serving dish or a couple of ramekins.

To make the topping, heat some olive oil in a frying pan (skillet), fry the pears until nice and golden, then add the sage leaves and thyme sprigs and allow to warm through.

Add the fried pears and herbs to the top of the pâté, then pour over the remainder of the olive oil from the pan to cover and encapsulate the topping. If there is not enough oil to cover the topping by 5 mm (¼ in), a little more olive oil.

Refrigerate the pâté for a couple of hours or overnight and wait for the top to solidify before serving.

INGREDIENTS

280 g (10 oz) pre-cooked brown
    lentils (I suggest cooking
    your own for this recipe following
    packet instructions; 140 g/5 oz
    dry weight)
1 yellow onion, sliced
4 garlic cloves, sliced
2 tablespoons olive oil, plus
    extra for frying and topping
300 g (10½ oz) chestnut mushrooms
1 tablespoon maple syrup
1 tablespoon tamari or soy sauce
1 tablespoon sherry
20 g (¾ oz) thyme leaves
salt and pepper, to taste

FOR THE TOPPING:

1 small pear, sliced lengthways
a few sage leaves
sprigs of thyme

GARLIC & HERB MACADAMIA CHEESE

A take on that classic French 80's cheese, Boursin. Superb on some white baguette or as an addition to your Christmas table layout. Taking the time to make this is definitely worth it.

MAKES
1 LARGE CHEESE OR
2 SMALLER ONES

INGREDIENTS

280 g (10 oz) macadamia nuts
160 ml (5½ fl oz/⅔ cup) water
2 tablespoons lemon juice and
    zest of 1 lemon
2 tablespoons snipped chives
1 garlic clove, grated
salt and pepper, to taste

TO SERVE:

fresh baguette or sourdough
    and some chutney
watercress sprigs

METHOD

Prepare the macadamia nuts by soaking them in a bowl of water for 2 hours – or even better do this the night before.

Drain the nuts and tip into a food processor or blender along with the water and blitz until smooth. (If you are using a small, hand-held blender, then blitz several times until smooth.) As this is a soft cheese the texture can be slightly bitty, which I personally love. If you are using a high-speed blender, make sure you don't overheat or overblend. You want the texture to be ricotta-like.

Once the nuts are blended, transfer to a clean glass container. Now it's time to flavour the cheese. Add the lemon juice and zest, chives, garlic, and salt and pepper, then mix well.

Use a metal chef's ring for this next step, if you have one. Alternatively, you can use a small bowl lined with cling film (plastic wrap). If you're using a chef's ring, place some greaseproof (waxed) paper under the ring and grease the inside with some oil. Fill the chef's ring or the bowl to the top with the cheese mixture.

Keep the cheese in the fridge for a few hours to set and let the flavours marry together.

Once chilled, pop the chef's ring off (if using) or remove the cheese from the bowl, and serve with some fresh baguette, French-style, or lovely sourdough, plus some chutney. The cheese will keep for up to 7 days in the fridge.

COOK'S TIP:

If you would like to age the cheese, transfer the blended macadamia to a bowl (not made from metal or it won't ferment), add the powder from half a probiotic capsule and mix well. Cover with a muslin cloth (cheesecloth) and keep outside the fridge for 24 hours to ferment. After 24 hours, the cheese will be slightly acidic in taste and have a thicker consistency.

NOT SAUSAGE ROLLS

/

A Christmas classic that anyone and everyone will like regardless of their food preferences. Great with some piccalilli or a cheeky dollop of ketchup, which is my personal favourite.

MAKES
8

METHOD

If you are using storebought pastry, then skip this first step. If you are making your own pastry, add the flour and curry powder to a large bowl. Chop the butter into small pieces and add to the flour mixture (you can grate the butter into the flour, if you wish). Use your fingers to rub the butter into the flour until well combined and crumbly in texture.

Add the water and vinegar and mix to bring the dough together into a smooth ball. Cover the bowl with cling film (plastic wrap) and place in the fridge to rest for 30 minutes.

While the dough is resting, make the filling. First blitz the walnuts and thyme in a food processor (make sure they still have a bit of bite).

Heat some olive oil in a medium saucepan, then fry the onion, garlic and mushrooms until the onion is translucent (a good 5 minutes). Add the blitzed walnuts and thyme, and fry for another 5 minutes.

Add the black beans, tamari/soy sauce, mustard, and salt and pepper. Remove from the heat and transfer to a bowl to cool.

Once cooled, add the oats and mash the mixture with your hands until you have a sticky consistency that holds together nicely.

Now to make the rolls. Place the dough on a clean floured surface, roll out to a rectangle measuring about 50 x 25 cm (20 x 10 in) and trim the edges.

INGREDIENTS

FOR THE PASTRY:

(You can also use ready-made puff pastry – a 320 g/11 oz packet will make 8 small rolls.)
390 g (14 oz/3⅛ cup) plain (all-purpose) flour, plus extra for dusting
1 teaspoon curry powder
240 g (8½ oz) cold vegan butter
180 ml (6 fl oz/¾ cup) cold water
1 teaspoon apple cider vinegar

FOR THE FILLING:

100 g (3½ oz) walnuts
4 sprigs of thyme, leaves picked
olive oil, for frying
1 large yellow onion, sliced
1 garlic clove, chopped
300 g (10½ oz) chestnut mushrooms, chopped
280 g (10 oz) tinned black beans, drained and rinsed
2 tablespoons tamari or soy sauce
1 tablespoon Dijon mustard
3 tablespoons rolled oats
vegan butter, melted, for brushing
sesame seeds, for sprinkling
salt and pepper, to taste

TO SERVE:

mustard
tomato ketchup
piccalilli

Brush the pastry lightly all over with melted butter, then arrange the filling along 50 cm (20 in) of the pastry, just off the centre. Fold the pastry over and use a fork to press the edges together.

Slice into 8 individual rolls using a sharp knife, then chill in the fridge for at least 30 minutes. The rolls will keep chilled for up to 24 hours, so are perfect to make ahead!

Preheat the oven to 220°C (430°F/gas 8) and arrange the rolls on a large baking tray (pan) lined with baking parchment.

Brush the rolls with more butter, sprinkle with a few pinches of sesame seeds and bake for 20 minutes. Remove the rolls from the oven, brush with more butter and cook for a further 10 minutes, or until golden brown.

Once the rolls are ready, leave to cool on a wire rack and serve warm with mustard, tomato ketchup and piccalilli.

SALT & PEPPER DEEP-FRIED BANANA BLOSSOM WITH RÉMOULADE SAUCE

SERVES
2

I have been cooking with banana blossoms for a while during my Retreat cheffing in places like Bali and Thailand. Accompanied by my fave rémoulade sauce, this works so well.

METHOD

To make the rémoulade, fry the shallot in some olive oil in a saucepan over a medium heat for 10 minutes until soft and translucent.

Add the remainder of the rémoulade ingredients to a bowl and mix well. Once the shallots are cooled, add to the bowl and stir them into the mix.

Pat the banana blossoms dry with some paper towel (they need to be very well dried for the best results).

Next make the batter by mixing together the chickpea flour, milk, apple cider vinegar, bicarbonate of soda, baking powder, chilli flakes, and salt and pepper in a bowl. The batter must be used immediately, otherwise the bicarbonate of soda will not be effective.

Heat a good amount of oil in a medium frying pan (skillet) to shallow-fry the banana blossoms. Once the oil is hot, grab each banana blossom at the bottom and dip in the batter. Fry on each side for around 2 minutes or until nice and crisp.

Once all the banana blossoms have been fried, rest them on some paper towel to soak up any excess oil, and serve immediately with a big dollop of rémoulade on top!

INGREDIENTS

400 g (14 oz) tin of banana blossom, drained and rinsed
80 g (3 oz/scant 1 cup) chickpea (gram) flour
110 ml (3½ fl oz/scant ½ cup) plant milk (I like oat milk)
1 teaspoon apple cider vinegar
⅛ teaspoon bicarbonate of soda (baking soda)
⅛ teaspoon baking powder
pinch of chilli (hot pepper) flakes
olive oil, for frying
pinch of salt and pepper

FOR THE RÉMOULADE:

1 shallot, chopped
olive oil, for frying
100 g (3½ oz/scant ½ cup) plant mayonnaise
1 tablespoon cornichons, chopped
1 tablespoon capers, chopped
1 teaspoon curry powder
small handful of dill fronds, chopped
salt and pepper, to taste

SMASHED BRUSSELS SPROUTS AND GARLIC MAYONNAISE

This is the only way to eat Brussels sprouts: crispy on the outside and nice and soft on the inside with extra crunch from the sesame seed addition. I am not a huge sprout lover, but I am a massive fan of these, especially dollop with a bit of mayo. You must make them!

MAKES
1 TRAY

INGREDIENTS

300–400 g (10½–14 oz)
    Brussels sprouts
olive oil, for cooking
sprinkle of white sesame seeds
salt and pepper, to taste

FOR THE GARLIC MAYONNAISE:

100 g (3½ oz/½ cup) plant
    mayonnaise
1 garlic clove, grated
juice of ½ a lemon
salt and pepper, to taste

METHOD

Preheat the oven to 220°C (430°F/430/gas 8).

Peel the outer layer of the sprouts and give them a good wash. Bring a large saucepan of salted water to the boil, add the sprouts and parboil for 10 minutes until semi-soft. Careful the sprouts don't turn a dull green which means they have been overcooked. Drain well.

Line a large baking tray (pan) with baking parchment, then spread the Brussels sprouts over the parchment. Make sure the sprouts have enough space in between and flatten them with the palm of your hand or the bottom of a drinking glass until they are as flat as possible. You might find that some water comes out of the sprouts when you flatten them, so soak up any excess water with paper towel.

Drizzle the sprouts with olive oil and a generous sprinkling of salt and sesame seeds, then pop in the oven for 10–15 minutes until brown.

Remove the tray from the oven, turn the sprouts, sprinkle with more sesame seeds and pop back in the oven for a further 10 minutes. You want the sprouts to be golden and crispy!

While the sprouts are cooking, mix all the ingredients for the mayonnaise together in a bowl and set aside.

Once the sprouts are golden, remove from the oven and eat immediately while they are super crispy, dipping them in the garlic mayo.

PLANT NUT ROAST WITH CAVOLO NERO
& APPLE AND CRANBERRY COMPOTE
—PAGE 138—

SLOW-ROASTED
SWEET RED CABBAGE
—PAGE 141—

MISO-ROASTED
POTATOES & ONIONS
—PAGE 140—

MAKE-AHEAD
GRAVY
—PAGE 143—

PICKLED
BRUSSELS SPROUTS
—PAGE 144—

PLANT NUT ROAST WITH CAVOLO NERO & APPLE AND CRANBERRY COMPOTE

This dish is brilliant in the sense that it is a proper centrepiece and can be enjoyed by all. It is equally as yummy the day after you make it and can also be transformed into a hash or squeezed between slices of bread for a sandwich.

METHOD

Cook the parsnips, swede and sweet potato in a large saucepan of boiling water for about 20 minutes or until tender. Drain well, then roughly mash.

Heat the oil in a large frying pan (skillet) and cook the leek, garlic and shallot for about 5 minutes until softened. Add the mushrooms, herbs and some salt and pepper, and fry for a further 5–10 minutes.

Preheat the oven to 220°C (430°F/gas 8).

Mix the vegetable mash, mushroom mixture, cooked rice, cavolo nero, ground almonds, walnuts and flax seeds together in a large bowl using a spatula until smooth.

Line a 900 g (2 lb) loaf pan with baking parchment, then add the mixture. You can also use a patterned, fancy, Christmas non-stick mould but I recommend brushing the inside with olive oil just for good measure (this cannot be lined with baking parchment as that would hide the pattern).

Reduce the temperature of the oven to 200°C (400°F/gas 6), then roast the loaf in the middle of the oven for about 40 minutes.

Remove the loaf from the oven, then lift out of the pan along with the paper (if using). Turn the loaf upside down onto a baking tray (pan) lined with baking parchment.

INGREDIENTS

2 parsnips (about 300 g/10½ oz), peeled and cut into 3–4 cm (1⅛–1½ in) pieces

½ small swede (rutabaga) (about 200 g/7 oz), peeled and cut into 3–4 cm (1⅛–1½ in) pieces

1 small sweet potato (about 150 g/5 oz), peeled and cut into 3–4 cm (1⅛–1½ in) pieces

1 tablespoon olive oil

1 small leek (about 160 g/5½ oz), washed and finely chopped

2 garlic cloves, chopped

1 small shallot, chopped

350 g (12 oz) mushrooms (such as chestnut or oyster), chopped

50 g (2 oz) herb leaves (such as rosemary, thyme and sage), finely chopped

120 g (4 oz/⅔ cup) cooked wholegrain rice (prepared according to the directions on packet)

200 g (7 oz) cavolo nero or kale, de-stemmed and roughly chopped

120 g (4 oz/1¼ cups) ground almonds (almond meal)

160 g (5½ oz) walnuts, chopped (plus an extra handful, toasted, to serve)

4 tablespoons cold-milled flaxseed

2 tablespoons tamari or soy sauce

1 tablespoon maple syrup

1 teaspoon Dijon mustard

salt and pepper, to taste

Mix the tamari/soy sauce with the maple syrup and mustard, then baste the loaf before returning to the oven to bake for a further 15–20 minutes.

To cook the cavolo nero accompaniment, massage the leaves with a little of the olive oil and a pinch of salt until soft. Preheat a medium frying pan (skillet), add a drizzle of olive oil and the garlic and fry the cavolo nero for 5 minutes. Add the tamari/soy sauce and sesame seed oil, then set aside.

To make the compote, add the apples, cranberries, ginger, maple syrup and lemon juice to a large saucepan, then pour in the water. Bring to the boil and simmer for 10–15 minutes until the mixture is soft and chunky, and all the liquid has been absorbed.

Once the nut roast is ready, allow to stand for 10 minutes before serving.

Serve on a platter with the sautéed cavolo nero and apple, cranberry and ginger compote, then top with some toasted walnuts.

SERVES
8

FOR THE SAUTÉED CAVOLO NERO:

200 g (7 oz) cavolo nero or kale, torn into small pieces and stalks discarded
1 tablespoon olive oil
pinch of salt
2 garlic cloves, chopped
2 tablespoons tamari or soy sauce
1 tablespoon toasted sesame seed oil

FOR THE APPLE AND CRANBERRY COMPOTE:

4 red apples (such as Braeburn or Royal Gala), unpeeled, cored and diced
100 g (3½ oz) fresh or frozen cranberries
3 cm (1⅛ in) piece of fresh root ginger, grated
1 tablespoon maple syrup
juice of 1 lemon
100 ml (3½ fl oz/scant ½ cup) water

MISO-ROASTED POTATOES & ONIONS

Patience is key to this dish. It is a great way to eat potatoes and onions married together with a miso basting oil, which brings sweetness and saltiness to two of my favourite ingredients.

SERVES
4–6

INGREDIENTS

4 large baking potatoes
3 large yellow onions
1 large garlic bulb

FOR THE BASTING OIL:

60 ml (2 fl oz/¼ cup) olive oil
2 tablespoons dark miso paste
1 tablespoon maple syrup
juice and zest of 1 lemon

FOR THE HERB CRUST:
1 piece of toast
1 teaspoon salt
pinch of pepper
1 garlic clove
10 g (½ oz) thyme, leaves removed

TOPPING:

2 spring onions (scallions),
    finely sliced

METHOD

Preheat the oven to 220°C (430°F/gas 8). Line a baking tray (pan) with baking parchment.

Peel and halve the potatoes and onions, then 'hedgehog' them by slicing through the top of each vegetable horizontally and vertically, to create a criss-cross effect.

Mix all the basting oil ingredients together in a bowl and set aside.

Blitz all the ingredients for the herb crust in a food processor or blender, then set aside.

Dip the onions and potatoes in the basting mix and cover well so that the mix gets into all the grooves.

Cook the potatoes and onions in the oven for 1½ hours in total, keeping them covered with aluminium foil for the first 30 minutes. After 30 minutes, turn the oven down to 200°C (400°F/gas 6), remove the foil and cook for a further 30 minutes. After this time, sprinkle the herb crust over the top of the potatoes and onions, then cook for a final 30 minutes.

Once the vegetables are ready, remove from the oven and sprinkle with the spring onions before serving.

COOK'S TIP:

Keep some of the basting mix in the bowl and use it to baste the vegetables every 15 minutes with a basting or pastry brush while the potatoes and onions are cooking.

SLOW-ROASTED SWEET RED CABBAGE

/

I make this at Christmas every year and have done for a while. Everyone who tries this recipe makes it a staple as it is such a great way to eat cabbage. The slow cooking process brings out the natural sweetness of the cabbage and this dish also keeps well in the fridge when made in a bigger batch.

SERVES
6

INGREDIENTS

1 small whole red cabbage
3 tablespoons olive oil
1 red onion, sliced
2 tablespoons tamari or soy sauce
2 tablespoons honey or maple syrup
30 g (1 oz) currants
pinch of cinnamon
salt and pepper, to taste

TOPPINGS:

2–3 spring onions (scallions),
    finely sliced
sprinkle of white sesame seeds

METHOD

Cut the cabbage in half down the middle and remove the hard core. Cut into thin slices.

Heat the olive oil in a large pan or wok (large enough to hold all the cabbage), then add the cabbage, onion, and salt and pepper. Start with a higher heat, as the salt will release liquid from the cabbage, then reduce to a low heat and cook down slowly for at least 30 minutes, stirring occasionally.

Once the cabbage mixture has cooked down and reduced in volume, it should be quite soft and sticky. Next add the tamari/soy sauce, honey/maple syrup, currants, cinnamon and more salt if necessary.

Mix well and place in a nice serving dish, topped with spring onions and sesame seeds.

MAKE-AHEAD GRAVY

MAKES 500 ML
[17 FL OZ/2 CUPS]

Everyone wants to get ahead during the holidays, so make this gravy in advance, then freeze it or keep it in the fridge until needed. I add a dollop of cream to mine in true Scandi style.

INGREDIENTS

20 g [¾ oz] dried or fresh shiitake mushrooms [dried mushrooms need soaking]

olive oil

1 large leek, washed thoroughly between the layers and chopped [green part and all]

4 celery stalks, roughly chopped

3 garlic cloves, roughly chopped

1 bay leaf

3–4 sprigs of thyme

3 tablespoons red wine, plus extra to taste

2 teaspoons dark miso paste

2 tablespoons balsamic vinegar

3 tablespoons tamari or soy sauce

4 tablespoons flour

1.25 litres [40 fl oz/4¾ cups] vegetable stock

1 tablespoon coconut cream or 3 tablespoons plant cream [optional]

METHOD

If you are using dried shiitake mushrooms, soak them in boiling water for 30–60 minutes [if you are using fresh mushrooms, you can skip this step). Roughly chop the mushrooms.

Preheat the oven to 200°C [400°F/gas 6].

Pour a good glug of olive oil into a large baking tray [pan], then add the leek, celery, garlic, herbs and mushrooms, mix well and cook in the oven for 20–30 minutes until nicely browned.

Remove the baking tray from the oven, add the red wine, miso paste, balsamic vinegar and tamari, and mix well.

Stir in the flour and pour in the stock, then heat on the stovetop to thicken, using a balloon whisk to stir frequently and prevent any lumps. I also like to add another glug of wine here and some extra tamari for good measure!

Once the gravy has thickened, strain through a sieve to remove any remaining lumps. You can use the gravy immediately or keep in a bowl or container and use later. The gravy also keeps in the freezer for a month to be used at a later date.

When you want to use the gravy, simply heat through in a saucepan before serving.

I like to add a splash of coconut or plant cream to my gravy, in true Scandi style, to make it just that bit thicker!

PICKLED
BRUSSELS SPROUTS

Have you ever pickled a sprout? If not,
I urge you to give this recipe a go. It is
easy, delicious and a great sweet and sour
condiment to go with heavier Christmas
dishes. This is one to make ahead and let
time do its thing.

MAKES ENOUGH
FOR A 1 KG
(2 LB 4 OZ) KILNER
(MASON) JAR

INGREDIENTS

600 g (1 lb 5 oz) Brussels sprouts
1 large shallot, peeled and very
    thinly sliced
150 g (5 oz/⅔ cup) caster
    (superfine) sugar
500 ml (17 fl oz/2 cups) raw
    organic apple cider vinegar
20 g (¾ oz) dill fronds, chopped
pinch of salt

METHOD

Sterilise a large Kilner jar (make sure this has an
accompanying rubber seal) by pouring a cup of boiling
water into the jar, putting the lid on and swirling the
water around. Empty the jar and set aside.

Prepare the Brussels sprouts by washing them well, then
chopping off the end bit and any dirty outer leaves (only
if they are not so nice). Cut each sprout in half and then
slice, but not too thinly.

Once all the sprouts are prepared, transfer to a large bowl
and pour in enough boiling water to cover them. Mix the
sprouts around in the water to ensure they are clean –
the boiling water will also blanch them slightly.

Drain the sprouts immediately (using a sieve sterilised with
boiling water) and add to the Kilner jar with the shallots.
Alternate the sprouts and shallots until the jar is filled.

Whisk the sugar, apple cider vinegar, dill and salt together
thoroughly in a bowl. Pour the mixture into the jar. If the
mixture doesn't reach the top of the jar, top up with a tiny
amount of boiling water.

Leave to cool, then keep in the back of the fridge and leave
for at least 1 week, until nice and crunchy and tangy with
a sweet and sour flavour.

CHOCOLATE ORANGE & AMARETTO MOUSSE

Very few ingredients are needed to make this incredibly light and satisfying mousse. It has an added grown-up twist of Amaretto, which can easily be skipped for little ones.

SERVES
4

METHOD

Add the coconut cream and all the other ingredients to a bowl. Use an electric hand-held whisk to mix everything together until fluffy (be careful not to overblend).

To make the caramelised oranges, heat the coconut oil in a small to medium saucepan and fry the orange slices before finishing off with the vanilla.

To serve, add a couple of caramelised orange slices to the bottom of each serving glass and spoon in the mousse. Top with grated chocolate and an orange slice (if using).

Refrigerate before serving or eat immediately.

INGREDIENTS

320 ml (11 fl oz/1⅓ cups)
    good-quality coconut cream
    or refrigerated full-fat tinned
    coconut milk (see *Cook's Tips*
    on page 148)
3 tablespoons runny peanut
    or almond butter
3 tablespoons cacao powder
2–3 tablespoons maple syrup
2 tablespoons Amaretto
zest of 1 orange

FOR THE CARAMELISED
ORANGES:

1 teaspoon of coconut oil
3 oranges, peeled and cut into slices
½ vanilla pod (bean), split and the
    seeds scraped out, or ½ teaspoon
    vanilla extract or paste

TO SERVE:

grated dark chocolate, with
    at least 70% cocoa solids
4 slices of orange (optional)

RISALAMANDE

This is a classic Danish Christmas dish that I have made into a plant-based version. Slow-cooked rice pudding is made extra luxurious with cream ladled in at the end and there's also a hidden almond for one lucky finder.

SERVES
4–6

METHOD

Boil the rice in the water in a medium saucepan until all the liquid has completely evaporated. This should take no more than 20–30 minutes.

Add the coconut cream, vanilla and sugar (or whichever sweetener you are using) to the rice and let everything simmer for a further 20 minutes until you have a beautiful, creamy, rice pudding-like consistency.

Once the rice pudding is ready let it cool down completely.

To finish, whip the cream and fold in to the rice pudding with the vanilla and cinnamon – and don't forget to add the almond.

Ladle into serving bowls, top with warm berries and basil, and whoever finds the lone almond in their dish has a lot of good luck coming their way!

COOK'S TIPS:

- Whatever quantity you would like to make, just use 1 part rice to 2 parts water to scale the recipe up or down.

- If using a fresh vanilla pod, once you have scraped out the seeds, pop the pod in the rice while it's cooking for extra flavour and remove before serving.

- If you would like to make *Whipped Coconut Cream* from coconut milk, see page 187.

INGREDIENTS

200 g (7 oz/1 cup) sushi rice (or any rice will do)
500 ml (17 fl oz/2 cups) water
250 ml (8½ fl oz/1 cup) coconut cream or refrigerated full-fat tinned coconut milk (see *Cook's Tips*)
½ vanilla pod (bean), split and the seeds scraped out, or ½ teaspoon vanilla paste or extract
2 tablespoons soft brown sugar or 1 tablespoon maple syrup, honey or coconut sugar
1 almond (to hide inside the pudding once cooked)

TO FINISH:

100 ml (3½ fl oz/scant ½ cup) coconut cream, whipped (see *Cook's Tips*)
½ vanilla pod (bean), split and the seeds scraped out (see *Cook's Tips*), or ½ teaspoon vanilla paste or extract

TO SERVE:

warmed berries (such as blueberries, blackberries and strawberries) and a sprinkling of ground cinnamon
basil sprigs

ICE CREAM YULE LOG

I am so proud of this one! This will tick everyone's boxes. Sweet, dense, indulgent and absolutely delish. Warning! You might have to make more than one of these over the holidays! Plus, it can be eaten frozen or just chilled.

SERVES
6–8

METHOD

Line a baking sheet with greaseproof (waxed) paper.

In a mixing bowl, whisk together the coconut cream, icing sugar, vanilla, nut butter and cacao powder (ideally using an electric whisk), until thick and mousse-like. Either refrigerate to use later or put in a piping bag if needed straightaway.

Pipe a 2 cm (¾ in) thick outline of chocolate mousse mixture on the baking sheet in the shape of the chocolate log you want to make, in this case an oval.

Arrange the Oreo cookies on their sides inside the outlined log, sticking them together with a squeeze of mousse between each one to act like a glue, until the shape is filled. You can add a row of cookies to the sides to make the chocolate log thicker if you wish.

Once the base is completely filled with Oreos, gently pipe more mousse over the top and sides, then smooth over with a palette knife at the end to make a yule log.

For the bark, chop the chocolate and sprinkle over the top of the log.

Blitz the cookies you kept to one side in a food processor or blender, then sprinkle over the chopped chocolate. Otherwise, just sprinkle the blended cookies directly over the top of the mousse.

The log can either be refrigerated and eaten as a mousse cake, or frozen and eaten as an ice-cream cake.

INGREDIENTS

FOR THE LOG:

480 ml (17 fl oz/scant 2 cups) good-quality coconut cream or refrigerated full-fat tinned coconut milk (see *Cook's Tips* on page 148)

80 g (3 oz/⅔ cup) icing (confectioner's) sugar

½ vanilla pod (bean), split and the seeds scraped out, or ½ teaspoon vanilla paste or extract

2 tablespoons runny nut butter

50 g (2 oz/½ cup) cacao powder

2 packets of Oreo cookies

FOR THE BARK:

100 g (3½ oz) dark chocolate, with at least 70% cocoa solids (optional)

2–3 Oreo cookies (from the packets used for the cake)

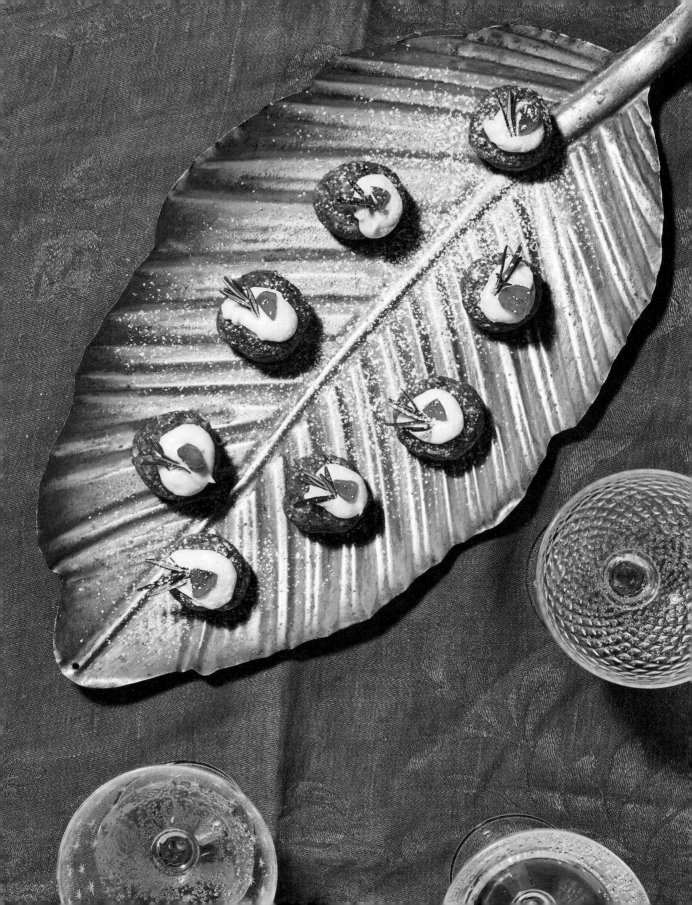

MINI CHRISTMAS CAKE BITES

MAKES
16

Making Christmas cake is such a time-consuming process. Don't get me wrong, I love Christmas cake, but I enjoy my time with family even more. This is a great recipe to make with loved ones or given as a gift.

INGREDIENTS

FOR THE CAKE BITES:

40 g (1½ oz/¾ cup) ground almonds (almond meal)
40 g (1½ oz) rolled oats
60 g (2 oz) pitted dates
200 g (7 oz) blanched almonds
50 g (2 oz) candied peel
50 g (2 oz) glacé (candied) cherries
50 g (2 oz) raisins
1 tablespoon orange marmalade
1 teaspoon ground cinnamon
1 teaspoon mixed spice
2 tablespoons whisky

FOR THE ICING:

100 g (3½ oz/¾ cup) icing (confectioner's) sugar
1 tablespoon water

TO DECORATE:

glacé (candied) cherries, chopped rosemary sprigs

METHOD

Add the ground almonds and oats to a food processor or blender and pulse to make a flour. Add the flour to a large bowl.

Put the dates, almonds, candied peel, glacé cherries, raisins, marmalade, cinnamon, mixed spice and whisky in a food processor or blender and mix until nicely incorporated.

Add the fruity mixture to the bowl of almond/oat flour and mix until well combined and feels sticky and mouldable.

Form the mixture into 16 small, bite-size balls and put on a plate lined with greaseproof (waxed) paper. Place in the fridge to firm up for 1 hour.

Meanwhile, make the icing by mixing the icing sugar and water into a paste.

Once the cake bites are ready, remove from the fridge and dip each one into the icing. Add a glacé cherry to the top of each bite and sprinkle with dried flower petals. These can be made for later or eaten straightaway.

SWEDISH
SAFFRON BREAD
—PAGE 156—

A MINCE PIE
—PAGE 158—

GLÖGG
—PAGE 159—

SWEDISH SAFFRON BREAD

This bread is a take on traditional Swedish Christmas buns, but is made in the shape of a *babka* with saffron and an almond, cinnamon and raisin filling. It's so good as a breakfast treat or an afternoon snack.

METHOD

Pour the milk into a saucepan, add the saffron and heat gently. Once heated, add the butter and stir to melt.

Remove the pan from the stovetop and leave to cool until the milk mixture is warm but not piping hot. A good way to test for this is to dip your finger in the mixture – it should feel warm but not burning. This is so the fresh yeast will be activated and dissolve well.

Once the mixture reaches a warm temperature, add the yeast and mix well, then add the sugar and stir until fully dissolved. Next add the yoghurt, orange zest and salt.

Transfer the mixture to a bowl and add the flour. Mix everything together well and then use the heel of your hand to knead the mixture until you have a nice dough ball. Once the dough has been worked and is slightly springy, leave in the bowl, cover with a dish towel and leave somewhere warm to rise for at least 30 minutes (or longer).

Preheat the oven to 180°C (350°F/gas 4).

While the bread is rising, make the filling. Blitz the ground almonds and sugar in a food processor or blender to combine. Put the mixture in a bowl, then add the butter, cinnamon, turmeric and raisins. Mix everything together and set aside.

INGREDIENTS

FOR THE BREAD:

250 ml (8½ fl oz/1 cup) plant milk
   (I like oat milk)
pinch of saffron
50 g (2 oz) vegan butter
25 g (1 oz) fresh yeast
80 g (3 oz/⅓ cup) caster
   (superfine) sugar
125 g (4 oz/½ cup) plant yoghurt
zest of 1 orange
pinch of salt
600 g (1 lb 6 oz) plain (all-purpose)
   flour, plus extra for dusting

FOR THE FILLING:

70 g (2½ oz/¾ cup) ground
   almonds (almond meal)
70 g (2½ oz/⅓ cup) caster
   (superfine) sugar
100 g (3½ oz) vegan butter, softened
1 teaspoon ground cinnamon
1 teaspoon ground turmeric
30 g (1 oz) raisins

Once the dough has risen, place on a clean floured surface and use a rolling pin to roll it into a rectangle (the longest side should be the same length as your loaf pan). Add the filling, roll the dough up horizontally, with the longest side facing you, then cut the roll in half along the long edge and braid it. You are aiming to create babka shape – a quick internet search will show you how to braid the bread.

Put the dough in a loaf pan lined with baking parchment and leave to rise again for another 30–40 minutes.

Bake in the oven for 45–60 minutes, until golden on top.

MAKES
1 LOAF

A MINCE PIE

/

My husband loves mince pies. Actually,
he is pretty obsessed with them. So, the
fact that he approved of this version is
win-win. This is a big mince pie rather than
lots of smaller ones, with a frangipane
topping to marry it all together.

*Note: The mincemeat needs to be made
in advance and kept in the fridge overnight.*

SERVES
6–8

METHOD

Chop the dried fruit with a knife before adding to a bowl.
Then add all the other mincemeat ingredients and mix
thoroughly. Keep in the fridge overnight.

To make the pastry, add all the dry ingredients to a bowl.
Chop the butter into small pieces and rub into the flour mix
with your hands. Add the milk, a little at a time, and mix
well to form a dough. Allow to rest somewhere warm for
15–20 minutes, or place in the fridge overnight.

Next day, when you're ready to make the pie, preheat the
oven to 180°C (350°F/gas 4). Grease a 21 cm (8 in) cake
or pie pan with a removable base with butter.

To make the frangipane topping, mix all the ingredients
together in a mixing bowl until well combined. Set aside.

Roll the pastry dough into a disc larger than the base of
the cake/pie pan, with enough to go up the sides of the pan.
Put the dough in the pan and press into the base and sides
so that the pastry lines the whole pan. Trim off any excess
dough that comes over the edge.

Prick the base of the pastry with a fork and pre-cook in the
oven for 10 minutes.

Remove the pie from the oven, fill with the mincemeat
(give it a good mix first), and press this down with the back
of your hand so it is nice and compact. Add the frangipane
mix on top and smooth flat with a palette knife.

Bake in the oven for 45 minutes.

INGREDIENTS

FOR THE MINCEMEAT:

375 g (13 oz) mixed dried fruit
1 large Bramley apple, peeled,
    cored and grated
100 ml (3½ fl oz/scant ½ cup) brandy
    (I love using Amaretto)
50 g (2 oz/¼ cup) dark brown sugar
10 g (½ oz) mixed peel
zest and juice of 1 lemon
zest and juice of 1 orange
pinch of ground nutmeg

FOR THE PASTRY:

250 g (9 oz/2 cups) plain
    (all-purpose) flour
pinch of salt
pinch of sugar
115 g (4 oz) vegan butter,
    plus extra for greasing
60 ml (2 fl oz/¼ cup) plant milk
    (I like oat milk)

FOR THE FRANGIPANE TOPPING:

170 g (6 oz/1¾ cups) ground
    almonds (almond meal)
100 g (3½ oz/½ cup) caster
    (superfine) sugar
50 g (2 oz/⅓ cup) plain
    (all-purpose) flour
1 teaspoon cornstarch (cornflour)
½ teaspoon baking powder
70 ml (2½ fl oz/5 tablespoons)
    plant milk
80 g (3 oz) vegan butter, melted
1 vanilla pod (bean), split and the
    seeds scraped out, or 1 teaspoon
    vanilla paste or extract

GLÖGG

Sweet, warm and spicy, *glögg*
(pronounced 'glue-gh') is Sweden's
seasonal mulled wine gift to chilly
souls around the globe. I really enjoy
it over the Christmas holidays, and
it brings back many happy memories.

SERVES
4–6

INGREDIENTS

200 ml (7 fl oz/scant 1 cup)
   apple juice
50 g (2 oz/¼ cup) soft brown sugar
2 cinnamon sticks
12 cardamom pods
12 whole cloves
zest and juice of 1 orange
60 ml (2 fl oz/¼ cup) Amaretto
1 bottle of red wine

OPTIONAL EXTRAS:

raisins
blanched almonds

METHOD

Mix all the ingredients (except for the red wine) in a bowl.
Leave to sit and infuse overnight.

The next day, pour the contents of the bowl into a saucepan
with the red wine and gently heat before serving. If you are
short of time, just simmer all the ingredients on a low heat
to infuse and then add the red wine to heat up at the end.

To serve, pass the glogg through a sieve to remove any whole
spices (you can pop these back in the remaining wine mix).
Then serve in pretty festive glasses with a few raisins and
almonds added (if using).

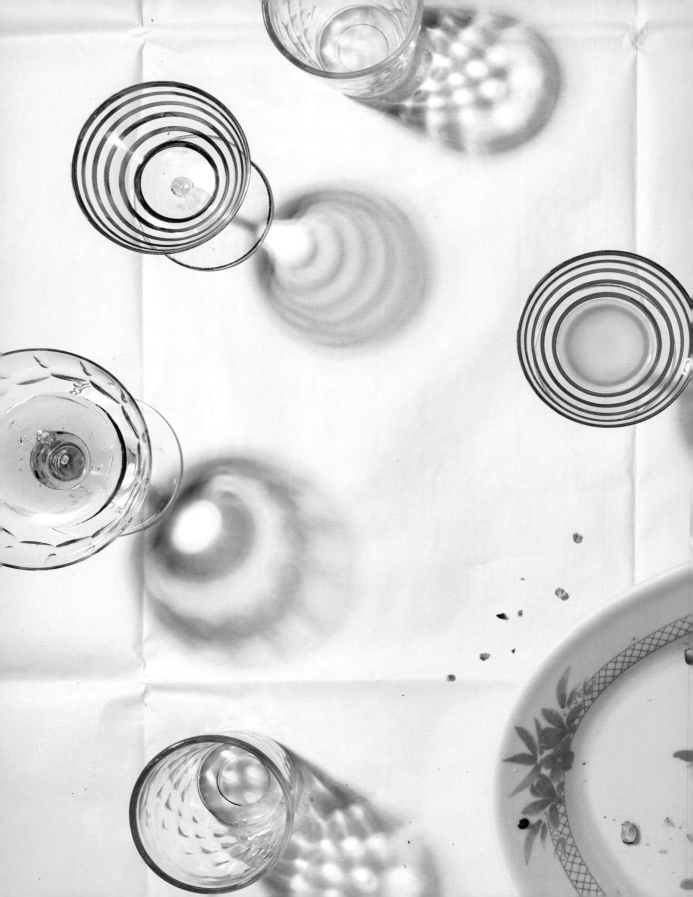

BIRTHDAY PARTIES

Birthday parties are so worth celebrating! The time and effort that it takes to put together a cake or a feast platter is an expression of love. I can't tell you how much I appreciate homemade birthday treats where you know the process is slightly time-consuming, but the result and reactions are always priceless.

THE ULTIMATE CHOCOLATE CAKE

/

⟲ ✿ ❄

SERVES 6–8

This cake is heavy, indulgent, slightly sticky and sweet, with a hint of saltiness. It works well for both children and adults, and it's truly one for all the chocolate lovers out there. In terms of toppings, you can be as sparse or as generous as you like, using cookie, chocolate or fruit toppings.

Note: Double the ingredients for the sponge and bake in two cake pans if you would like a taller cake. You will also need to double the quantity of chocolate mousse topping to cover the bigger cake. There is also a gluten-free version of this cake in the Make Your Own chapter, page 186.

METHOD

Before making the cake, soften the dates for the salted caramel filling by soaking them in a bowl filled with boiling water for 10–15 minutes. Drain and set aside.

Preheat the oven to 180°C (350°F/gas 4). Grease a 21 cm (8 in) springform cake pan with butter (you can also use coconut oil) or two, if you are doubling.

To make the cake, cream the butter and sugar together in a large bowl until soft and fluffy.

In another bowl, whisk the aquafaba until it is white, fluffy and forming stiff peaks. This will take a good 10 minutes. Use an electric whisk as this makes it much easier! Set aside.

Add the milk to a saucepan and bring to the boil. Remove from the heat, then add the chocolate pieces and stir through the milk until melted.

Add the flour, cacao powder, bicarbonate of soda, baking powder, apple cider vinegar, vanilla, and salt to the large bowl. Add the chocolate milk slowly and mix well until everything is well incorporated.

Lastly, gently fold in the whipped aquafaba and pour the mixture into the cake pan.

Bake in the oven for 30–40 minutes.

Continues overleaf

INGREDIENTS

FOR THE CHOCOLATE CAKE:

150 g (5 oz) vegan butter,
  plus extra for greasing
150 g (5 oz/¾ cup) soft brown sugar
3 tablespoons aquafaba
  (liquid from tinned chickpeas)
250 ml (8½ fl oz/1 cup) plant milk
  (I like oat milk)
150 g (5 oz) good-quality, dairy-free
  dark chocolate, with at least
  70% cocoa solids, broken into
  small pieces
250 g (9 oz/2 cups) self raising flour
3 tablespoons cacao powder
2 teaspoons baking powder
1 tablespoon apple cider vinegar
1 vanilla pod (bean), split and the
  seeds scraped out, or 1 teaspoon
  vanilla paste or extract
pinch of salt

FOR THE SALTED CARAMEL
FILLING:

200 g (7 oz) Medjool dates, pitted
200 ml (7 fl oz/scant 1 cup) water
  (use the water from soaking
  the dates)
2 tablespoons peanut butter
  (or any nut butter will do)
pinch of salt

Continues overleaf

Check if the cake is ready by inserting a skewer into the middle and seeing if it comes out clean (it may need an extra 5–10 minutes). Remove the cake from the oven and place on a wire rack to cool completely.

To make the filling, add the soaked dates to a food processor or blender along with the soaking water, peanut butter and salt, and blitz until smooth.

Once the cake has cooled completely, pop it out of the cake pan. Slice in half horizontally, spread the salted caramel filling over the lower half of the cake, then place the other half on top. (If you are making a double-decker cake, sandwich together the two larger layers made in separate cake pans.)

To make the avocado mousse topping, blitz all the ingredients together in a food processor or blender until smooth. Smooth the mousse over the top and down the sides of the cake until fully covered. Use a piping bag for a fancier finish.

If you choose to make the coconut-based mousse, add all the ingredients into a bowl and mix with a food processor or blender until smooth.

To decorate the cake, sprinkle with grated chocolate or cover with chocolate buttons, Oreos, fruit or any other indulgent toppings you like.

COOK'S TIPS:

- Don't let any salted caramel leftovers go to waste – just put the chocolate mousse ingredients straight into the food processor or blender you used for the caramel and save on washing up!

- If you use a vanilla pod, pop the empty pod (once you have scraped out the seeds for the recipe) in your sugar bowl to give a lovely vanilla hint to the sugar.

FOR THE CHOCOLATE
MOUSSE TOPPING
(AVOCADO BASED):

1 large or 2 small avocados
50 g (2 oz/½ cup) cacao powder
60 ml (2 fl oz/¼ cup) maple syrup

FOR THE CHOCOLATE
MOUSSE TOPPING
(COCONUT BASED):

560 g (20 oz) coconut cream
250 g (9 oz) runny peanut butter
50 g (2 oz/½ cup) cacao powder
60 ml (2 fl oz/¼ cup) maple syrup

SUGGESTED TOPPINGS:

grated chocolate
chocolate buttons
Oreo cookies
selection of fruits and berries

GIANT CHOCOLATE COOKIE

/

Who doesn't love cookies? Especially a huge, chocolate-stuffed one? This cookie also only takes minutes to make. It has great wow factor and will make anyone instantly happy. You can play around with optional fillings and toppings according to taste.

METHOD

Preheat the oven to 180°C (350°F/gas 4). Line a baking tray (pan) with baking parchment.

Whisk the aquafaba in a bowl until it is white, fluffy and forming soft peaks. This will take at least 10 minutes. I find an electric whisk makes this much easier. Set aside.

Cream the butter, caster sugar and dark brown sugar together in another bowl until soft and fluffy. Add the flour, cacao powder, bicarbonate of soda, vanilla and salt, and mix well until combined. Then gently fold in the aquafaba.

Divide the mixture equally and then roll it between your hands to make two nice round balls of dough.

On a baking tray (pan), place the first ball on the baking parchment and press down to create a giant round cookie, 1 cm (½ in) thick and place the dough between two sheets of greaseproof (waxed) paper and roll it out with a rolling pin.

Spread the chocolate chips evenly over the top of the cookie.

Make another giant round cookie with the other half of the mixture, and place on top of the layer of chocolate chips. Seal the sides by pinching the top and bottom cookies together at the edges. Add more chocolate chips, nuts or sprinkles for good measure.

Bake in the oven for 12 minutes. Serve warm or cold.

SERVES 4–6

INGREDIENTS

4 tablespoons aquafaba (liquid from tinned chickpeas)
160 g (5½ oz) vegan butter, softened
80 g (3 oz/⅓ cup) caster (superfine) sugar
2 tablespoons dark brown sugar
170 g (6 oz/1 ⅓ cups) plain (all-purpose) flour
6 tablespoons cacao powder
½ teaspoon bicarbonate of soda (baking soda)
½ vanilla pod (bean), split and the seeds scraped out, or ½ teaspoon vanilla paste or extract
pinch of salt
150 g (5 oz) chocolate chips (any type you prefer), with a few saved for the topping
chopped nuts or sprinkles, to top (optional)

FRUIT SUSHI WITH CHOCOLATE
& STRAWBERRY DIPPING SAUCE
—PAGE 168—

GIANT CHOCOLATE
COOKIE
—PAGE 169—

FRUIT SUSHI WITH CHOCOLATE & STRAWBERRY DIPPING SAUCE

This is such a great little recipe to make with children. Not only is it delicious, but also easy to make, and it includes some great ingredients and colourful options. The rice pudding can be made ahead of time – as can all the components – so all you need to do is put everything together before serving.

METHOD

To make the rice pudding, rinse the rice thoroughly under cold water and add to a saucepan of already boiling water. Stir frequently until the rice is cooked.

When the rice is soft and the water has evaporated (about 15 minutes), add the sugar, vanilla and coconut cream, and mix well. Simmer until the rice mixture is nice and thick, about 5 more minutes. Remove from the heat, replace the lid on the pan and set aside to cool down fully. To cool more quickly, transfer to another container.

Once the rice pudding has cooled down completely, you can start preparing the fillings. Think of these as sushi rolls, which means you need to cut your choice of fruits into strips where possible – you can leave pomegranates and blueberries whole, for example, and just slice the strawberries.

Now for the assembly. Add enough hot water to a large, round plate or a vessel larger than the rice paper sheets, so you can dip/cover a full sheet.

Dip the rice paper sheets one at a time in the hot water for a few seconds only, to soften.

INGREDIENTS

1 packet of rice paper rolls (10 sheet)
200 g (7 oz) fresh fruit (such as strawberries, mango, pineapple, berries, bananas and pomegranates)
a few mint leaves (for a more grown-up touch)

FOR THE RICE PUDDING FILLING:

150 g (5 oz/¾ cup) sushi rice
300 ml (10 fl oz/1¼ cups) boiling water
1 tablespoon soft brown sugar
1 vanilla pod (bean), split and the seeds scraped out, or 1 teaspoon vanilla paste or extract
2 tablespoons coconut cream

FOR THE CHOCOLATE DIPPING SAUCE:

1 bar of your favourite chocolate bar (melted)
1–2 teaspoons coconut oil

FOR THE STRAWBERRY DIPPING SAUCE:

200 g (7 oz) strawberries, de-stemmed
1 tablespoon coconut oil
dash of maple syrup (optional)
sprinkle of vanilla seeds from a split vanilla pod/bean (optional)

Place the sheets flat on a clean surface and add a few slices of fruit to the bottom that way you will have a lovely fruit pattern and a few tablespoons of the rice pudding mixture and some strawberry slices (or your preferred fruit) to the middle. You can also add a few sprigs of mint (although children might prefer their rolls without).

Make the sushi roll by folding the edge of rice paper that's closest to you over the filling, then fold in each side and finally fold the furthest edge in towards you (just like folding a burrito). Set aside on a separate plate. Repeat for each individual roll.

To make the chocolate dipping sauce, melt your favourite bar of chocolate in a bain-marie. To make the sauce runnier, add 1–2 teaspoons of coconut oil and stir through the melted chocolate.

To make the strawberry dipping sauce, blitz the strawberries and coconut oil in a high-speed blender. The oil emulsifies with the strawberries to form a lovely, creamy, light dipping sauce.

Serve the fruit sushi on a big platter, either whole or cut in half, along with the two dipping sauces.

COOK'S TIP:

The hot water for dipping should act like a glue that sticks the edges together. You may need to top up the hot water as you go because it will cool down. Make sure you take your time – dip each rice paper sheet separately and don't put more than one in the water in one go!

MAKES
10 LARGE ROLLS

SPONGE
& SPRINKLES

This is the ultimate homage to my childhood. You simply can't go wrong with a vanilla sponge, white icing and sprinkles on top. This cake is popular with children and adults alike and is a joy to make and serve. I mean who doesn't love sprinkles? They make everyone happy!

Note: Double the ingredients for the sponge and bake in two sandwich cake pans if you would like to make a bigger double-decker cake. You will also need to double the quantity of icing to cover the bigger cake.

SERVES
6–8

METHOD

Preheat the oven to 180°C (350°F/gas 4). Grease a 21 cm (8 in) springform cake pan with butter (you can also use coconut oil). A square cake pan also works nicely for this cake.

To make the cake, cream the butter and sugar together in a large bowl until soft and fluffy.

In another bowl, whisk the aquafaba until it is white, fluffy and forming stiff peaks. This will take a good 10 minutes. I find an electric whisk makes this much easier! Set aside.

Add the flour, baking powder, milk, apple cider vinegar, vanilla, and salt to the large bowl. Mix to incorporate everything well.

Gently fold the aquafaba through the mix, then pour into the prepared cake pan. Bake in the oven for 40 minutes.

Check if the cake is ready by inserting a skewer into the middle and seeing if it comes out clean (it may need an extra 5–10 minutes). Remove the cake from the oven and place on a wire rack to cool completely.

While the cake is cooling, make the icing by mixing the butter, yoghurt and sugar together in a bowl.

When the cake has cooled, remove from the cake pan and slice in half horizontally. (If you are making a double-decker cake, sandwich together the two larger layers made in separate cake pans.)

INGREDIENTS

FOR THE CAKE:

120 g (4 oz) vegan butter,
    plus extra for greasing
150 g (5 oz/⅔ cup) caster (superfine)
    sugar
3 tablespoons aquafaba (liquid
    from tinned chickpeas)
320 g (11¼ oz/2½ cups)
    self-raising flour
2 teaspoons baking powder
300 ml (10 fl oz/scant 1¼ cups)
    plant milk (I like oat milk)
1 tablespoon apple cider vinegar
1 vanilla pod (bean), split and the
    seeds scraped out, or 1 teaspoon
    vanilla paste or extract
pinch of salt

FOR THE ICING:

90 g (3 oz) vegan butter
2 tablespoons thick plant yoghurt
100 g (3½ oz) icing (confectioner's)
    sugar
1 big packet of multi-coloured
sprinkles

FOR THE INSIDE LAYER:

1 jar of strawberry or raspberry jam
    (about 340 g/12 oz)
1 punnet (tray) of strawberries
    (about 250 g/9 oz),
    de-stemmed and sliced

Place the bottom half on a serving platter and spread with a layer of jam followed by a layer of strawberries. Pop the other half of the cake on top, cover the top and sides with icing, and decorate generously with lots of sprinkles!

PINK BISCUIT CAKE

/

This is another nod to my childhood, but this time it is to my Bulgarian grandmother who used to make a type of biscuit cake with fluorescent-pink custard. I have selfishly recreated this recipe, which can be made in a beautiful glass vessel, oven dish, cake pan or individual glasses to show off each layer. It is a great make-ahead dessert as well.

SERVES
6–8

METHOD

Add the cornflour, milk, vanilla and sugar to a saucepan and whisk together over a medium heat. Keep whisking until the mixture begins to boil and thickens like a traditional custard. Make sure the custard mixture doesn't boil over! The mixture is thick enough when it coats the back of a spoon. Remove from the heat and set aside.

Blitz the chopped strawberries in a food processor or blender until you have a smooth purée. Add to the mixture in the pan and stir to combine and turn the custard pink.

Cover the base of an oven dish (preferably made from glass so you can see the layers) with a layer of pink custard, then add a layer of biscuits to cover the custard.

Add dollops of jam sporadically over the biscuits, and repeat with more layers of custard, biscuits and jam until all the ingredients are used up, finishing with a layer of custard.

Set aside to cool and then refrigerate for at least 2 hours to allow the cake to set.

Just before serving, whip the cream in a bowl and remove the cake from the fridge. Top the cake with the whipped cream and your choice of fresh berries.

INGREDIENTS

FOR THE CAKE:

4 generous tablespoons cornflour (cornstarch)
1 litre (34 fl oz/4 cups) plant milk (I like oat milk)
1 vanilla pod (bean), split and the seeds scraped out, or 1 teaspoon vanilla paste or extract
2 tablespoons soft brown sugar
220 g (8 oz) strawberries, de-stemmed and roughly chopped
2 x 120 g (4 oz) packets of plain tea biscuits (gluten-free, if you prefer)
1 jar of strawberry jam (about 340 g/12 oz)

FOR THE TOPPING:

200 ml (7 fl oz/scant 1 cup) whippable plant cream
handful of fresh berries (such as strawberries, raspberries and blackberries)

FRUIT CHOCOLATE POPSICLES WITH PISTACHIOS

This is a very healthy way of creating delicious party treats using the natural beauty and sweetness of fruits combined with melted chocolate and the added crunch of nut and seed toppings. A great option for summer parties and loved by both children and grown-ups.

SERVES
6–8

INGREDIENTS

1 watermelon (you can also use pineapple, mango, strawberries, bananas and clementine wedges)
wooden popsicle sticks

FOR THE CHOCOLATE DRIZZLE:

120 ml (4 fl oz/½ cup) coconut oil
60 ml (2 fl oz/¼ cup) maple syrup
50 g (2 oz/½ cup) cacao powder (or melt any leftover chocolate bars you may have).

TOPPING:

30 g (1 oz) pistachios, chopped
40 g (1¼ oz) pomegranate seeds

METHOD

Line a baking tray (pan) with greaseproof (wax) paper.

Cut the watermelon horizontally into large, pizza-shaped circles, about 2.5 cm (1 in) thick, then cut these into triangles. You will get four to six pieces out of each round.

Make a small incision in the bottom of each triangle (where the skin is) and insert the popsicle stick. You can also do this for other fruits you are using – in fact, it's nice to have a selection of fruits to choose from. (For softer fruits like strawberries, mango and banana, there's no need to make an incision in the skin first.)

Freeze the fruit popsicles for at least 1 hour.

While the popsicles are in the freezer, you can make the chocolate drizzle and chop up the pistachios for the topping. Simply melt the coconut oil in a saucepan or microwave, then add all the ingredients to a bowl and mix until smooth.

Remove the popsicles from the freezer. Dip the fruit in the chocolate drizzle or just drizzle on top, lay the popsicles on the greaseproof paper and sprinkle all over with pistachios and pomegranate seeds. Keep refrigerated until you're ready to serve.

These popsicles look great arranged on a nice platter and are wonderful eaten on a hot summer's day.

MINI CHOCOLATE CUPCAKES WITH CREAM & BERRIES

These little gems are perfect portion sized chocolate cupcakes. Fluffy, soft and delicious dolloped with cream and berries. So simple to make and yet satisfying to taste and look at. These cakes can also easily be made gluten-free.

METHOD

Preheat the oven to 180°C (350°F/gas 4). Place 12 cupcake cases in a muffin tray (pan).

Cream the butter and sugar together in a large bowl until soft and fluffy. Add the remainder of the ingredients and mix to incorporate fully.

Using an ice-cream scoop, distribute the mixture evenly between the cupcake cases. Bake in the oven for 12 minutes.

Remove the cakes from the oven and set aside to cool. They will sink slightly and may seem underdone, but that is how they are supposed to be.

To make the topping, whip the plant cream and then mix in the vanilla and maple syrup.

Once the cakes have cooled, top with the whipped cream and decorate with berries, chocolate shavings or other toppings of your choice.

INGREDIENTS

FOR THE CAKES:

100 g (3½ oz) vegan butter
100 g (3½ oz/½ cup) soft brown
    sugar
200 ml (7 fl oz/scant 1 cup)
    plant milk (I like oat milk)
100 g (3½ oz/½ cup) self raising flour
    (for a gluten-free version,
    use 100 g/3½ oz/1¼ cups self
    raising gluten-free flour mix)
1 tablespoon apple cider vinegar
1 teaspoon baking powder
6 tablespoons cacao powder
pinch of salt

FOR THE CREAM TOPPING:

150 ml (5 fl oz/scant ⅔ cup)
    whippable plant cream
    (I like oat cream)
½ teaspoon vanilla paste or extract
1 tablespoon maple syrup

TO DECORATE:

handful of berries
    (or fruit of your choice)
chocolate shavings

SAVOURY SWEDISH SANDWICH CAKE

Growing up in Sweden this was my grandmother's speciality. Traditionally made with seafood or charcuterie, this version is a celebration of plant-based fillings and toppings. It is ideal for people such as me who prefer savoury over sweet, but still want to feel that a lot of effort and love has gone into creating a brilliant savoury cake option.

METHOD

Make the hummus filling by adding all the ingredients (except the beetroot and spinach) to a food processor or blender and blitzing until smooth.

Split the hummus equally between two bowls. Put the hummus from one of the bowls back in the food processor/blender, add the beetroot and blitz to create a lovely purple beetroot hummus. Set aside.

Mix the spinach in the other bowl of hummus and then blitz in the food processor/blender to make a green spinach hummus. Set aside.

To make the tofu 'icing', blitz the tofu, nutritional yeast, lemon juice, salt and pepper in a food proccessor or blender. Pour into a bowl and mix in the chives and mayonnaise (if you are using tofu).

Cover a large, flat platter with 2–3 pieces of bread to create a rectangular surface (or a square one if you are using a square platter). If the shape isn't perfect, you can cut the middle piece of bread to fit.

Spread a generous layer of beetroot hummus over the first layer of bread, right up to the edges. Add another layer of bread and then a layer of spinach hummus. At this point, add any optional filling on top, before adding another layer of bread.

Keep adding layers (approximately 3–4 in total) until the fillings are used up. Make sure all the gaps are filled (just like icing between traditional cake layers).

INGREDIENTS

1 loaf of sliced sandwich bread
(gluten-free, if you prefer)

FOR THE HUMMUS FILLING:
(the glue that holds everything together)

2 x 400 g (14 oz) tins of chickpeas,
drained and rinsed
3 tablespoons tahini
juice of 1 lemon
2 garlic cloves
2 tablespoons olive oil
240 ml (8½ fl oz/1 cup) hot water
pinch of salt and pepper
1 cooked beetroot bulb,
peeled and grated
handful of spinach leaves

ADDITIONAL FILLING OPTIONS
(SLICED):

plant feta
smoked tofu (I prefer organic)
gherkins
avocado
pickled beetroot
capers

FOR THE SAVOURY 'ICING':

500 g (1 lb 2 oz) tofu
(I prefer organic) or plant
cream cheese or mayonnaise
1 tablespoon nutritional yeast
(this is deactivated yeast)
juice of ½ lemon
pinch of salt and pepper
20 g (¾ oz) chives, snipped,
plus extra to garnish
1 tablespoon plant mayonnaise
(if you are using tofu)

Once the layers are finished, spread the tofu icing over the top and down the sides of the cake. For a neater finish, use a piping (pastry) bag.

Next, stand lettuce leaves upright all around the edges of the cake – they will stick to the icing, which will hold them in place.

Sprinkle the top of the cake with more chives and decorate with slices of avocado and lemon, or any of the other decoration options.

COOK'S TIPS:

- Keep the liquid from the tins of chickpeas to use as aquafaba, which appears in lots of the other recipes in this book.

- If you want a perfect shape, you can cut the crusts off the pieces of bread. However, for zero waste, I keep them on.

- There's a lovely Swedish furniture shop that happens to sell vegan caviar, which looks great sprinkled on top.

TO GARNISH:

2 baby gem lettuce heads
1 ripe avocado,
   peeled and sliced
lemon slices
cucumber slices
cherry tomatoes
seaweed caviar
   (optional; see *Cook's Tip*)

MAKE YOUR OWN

Here is a small chapter
of basic recipes. There is
a standard custard used
through out the book.
An almond cheese that
lends itself to many versions
along with gluten free cake
options so that everyone
can join in the celebrations.

MAKES
1 JAR

ALMOND FETA

This is the basic recipe for almond feta which features in some of the recipes in the book.

METHOD

Soften the almonds first by soaking them in a bowl of water for 2 hours.

After 2 hours, drain and rinse the almonds, then tip into a food processor or blender along with the water and pinch of salt, and blitz until you have a smooth texture.

Once the almonds are blended, either age the cheese (see *Cook's Tip*) or flavour with salt. Be generous, as cheese should be salty. If you are ageing the cheese, then flavour with salt after the 24-hour ageing period.

Once salted, wrap the cheese mixture in a piece of muslin cloth (cheesecloth), create a tight ball and place in a sieve for steadiness. Place the sieve over a bowl, then add something heavy on top to weigh down the ball and push out any excess liquid. Keep in the fridge overnight.

The feta cheese will last for up to 7 days in the fridge in an airtight container.

INGREDIENTS

280 g (10 oz) blanched almonds
160 ml (5½ fl oz/⅔ cup) water
pinch of salt, plus extra for seasoning
½ probiotic capsule (optional)

COOK'S TIP: If you would like to age the cheese, transfer the blended almonds to a bowl (not made from metal or it won't ferment), add the powder from half a probiotic capsule and mix well. Cover with a muslin cloth (cheesecloth) and keep outside the fridge for 24 hours to ferment. After 24 hours, the cheese will be slightly acidic in taste and have a thicker consistency.

SERVES
4 – 6

HOMEMADE CUSTARD

I love custard! You will see that custard features in many of my recipes and is often the glue that holds cakes and desserts together.

METHOD

Whisk the cornflour/custard powder, milk, turmeric, vanilla and sugar together in a small saucepan.

Bring to the boil on the stovetop while stirring until the custards thickens enough to coat the back of a spoon, then remove from the heat.

Stir in the lemon zest and set aside to cool.

INGREDIENTS

2 tablespoons cornflour (cornstarch) or 2 tablespoons dairy-free custard powder

360 ml (12 fl oz/1½ cups) whole plant milk (I prefer full-fat oat milk)

¼ teaspoon ground turmeric

1 vanilla pod (bean), split and the insides scraped out, or 1 teaspoon vanilla paste or extract

2 tablespoons caster (superfine) sugar or a sweetener of your choice

zest of ½ lemon

VANILLA SPONGE CASE BASE

This classic sponge is used throughout the book. From the tiramisù recipe on page 29 to the layered trifle on page 100, it's a great base recipe that works in many ways.

SERVES
6–8

INGREDIENTS

120 g (4 oz) vegan butter,
 plus extra for greasing
150 g (5 oz/⅔ cup) caster (superfine)
 sugar (caster sugar keeps the
 cake light and airy)
3 tablespoons aquafaba
 (liquid from tinned chickpeas)
320 g (11¼ oz/2½ cups)
 self raising flour
1 teaspoon baking powder
300 ml (10½ fl oz/scant 1 cup)
 plant milk (I like oat milk)
1 tablespoon apple cider vinegar
1 vanilla pod (bean), split and the
 insides scraped out, or 1 teaspoon
 vanilla paste or extract
pinch of salt

METHOD

Preheat the oven to 180°C (350°F/gas 4). Grease a 21 cm (8 in) springform cake pan with butter or coconut oil.

In a large bowl, cream the butter and sugar together until soft and fluffy.

In another bowl, whisk the aquafaba until it is white, fluffy and forming stiff peaks. This will take a good 10 minutes. I find using an electric whisk makes this much easier! Set aside.

Add the flour, baking powder, milk, apple cider vinegar, vanilla and salt to the large bowl of creamed butter and sugar. Mix to incorporate everything well.

Gently fold the aquafaba through the mixture, then pour into the prepared cake pan.

Bake the cake in the oven for 40–50 minutes. Check if the cake is ready by inserting a skewer into the middle and seeing if it comes out clean (it may need an extra 5–10 minutes).

Remove the cake from the oven and place on a wire rack to cool completely. Once fully cooled, pop the cake out of the pan.

GLUTEN-FREE VANILLA SPONGE CAKE

This is the classic vanilla sponge cake,
but a gluten-free version.

SERVES
6–8

METHOD

Preheat the oven to 180°C (350°F/gas 4). Grease a 21 cm
(8 in) springform cake pan with butter or coconut oil.

In a large bowl, cream the butter and sugar together
until soft and fluffy.

In another bowl, whisk the aquafaba until it is white,
fluffy and forming stiff peaks. This will take a good
10 minutes. I find using an electric whisk makes this
much easier! Set aside.

Blitz the apple and milk in a food processor or blender
to form a purée.

Add the flour, bicarbonate of soda, baking powder, apple
and milk purée, apple cider vinegar, vanilla and salt to the
large bowl of creamed butter and sugar. Mix to incorporate
everything well.

Gently fold the aquafaba through the mixture, then pour
into the prepared cake pan.

Bake in the oven for 40–50 minutes. Check if the cake is
ready by inserting a skewer into the middle and seeing
if it comes out clean (it may need an extra 5–10 minutes).

Remove the cake from the oven and place on a wire rack
to cool completely. Once fully cooled, pop the cake out
of the pan.

INGREDIENTS

120 g (4 oz) vegan butter,
   plus extra for greasing
150 g (5 oz/⅔ cup) caster (superfine)
   sugar (caster sugar keeps the
   cake light and airy)
3 tablespoons aquafaba
   (liquid from tinned chickpeas)
1 small apple, peeled, cored
   and chopped
240 ml (8½ fl oz/1 cup) plant milk
   (I like oat milk)
320 g (11¼ oz/2½ cups) gluten-free
   self-raising flour
½ teaspoon bicarbonate of soda
   (baking soda)
2 teaspoons baking powder
1 tablespoon apple cider vinegar
1 vanilla pod (bean), split and the
   insides scraped out, or 1 teaspoon
   vanilla paste or extract
pinch of salt

CLASSIC GLUTEN-FREE CHOCOLATE CAKE

This is a classic chocolate sponge cake,
but a gluten-free version.

SERVES
6–8

METHOD

Preheat the oven to 180°C (350°F/gas 4). Grease a 21 cm
(8 in) springform cake pan with butter or coconut oil.

In a large bowl, cream the butter and sugar together
until soft and fluffy.

In another bowl, whisk the aquafaba until it is white,
fluffy and forming stiff peaks. This will take a good
10 minutes. I find using an electric whisk makes this
much easier! Set aside.

Add the milk to a saucepan and bring to the boil. Remove
from the heat, then add the chocolate and stir through
the milk to melt.

Add the flour, cacao powder, bicarbonate of soda, baking
powder, chocolate milk (slowly), apple cider vinegar,
vanilla, carrot and salt to the bowl of creamed butter
and sugar. Mix to incorporate everything well.

Lastly, gently fold the aquafaba through the mixture,
then pour into the prepared cake pan.

Bake in the oven for 45 minutes. Check if the cake is ready
by inserting a skewer into the middle and seeing if it comes
out clean (it may need an extra 5–10 minutes).

Remove the cake from the oven and place on a wire rack
to cool completely. Once fully cooled, pop the cake out
of the pan.

INGREDIENTS

150 g (5 oz) vegan butter,
  plus extra for greasing
150 g (5 oz/¾ cup) soft brown sugar
3 tablespoons aquafaba
  (liquid from tinned chickpeas)
360 ml (12 fl oz/1½ cups) plant milk
  (I like oat milk)
150 g (5 oz) good-quality, dairy-free
  dark chocolate, with 70% cocoa
  solids, broken into small pieces
250 g (9 oz/2 cups) self raising
  gluten-free white flour
3 tablespoons cacao powder
½ teaspoon bicarbonate of soda
  (baking soda)
2 teaspoons baking powder
1 tablespoon apple cider vinegar
1 vanilla pod (bean), split and the
  insides scraped out, or 1 teaspoon
  vanilla paste or extract
1 carrot, peeled, chopped, boiled,
  and puréed (you need 120 g/
  4 oz purée)
pinch of salt

WHIPPED
COCONUT CREAM

Coconut cream is the new 'cream' on the block. It's great in desserts and fantastic whipped. The best way to make whipped coconut cream is to buy tinned or Tetra-packed coconut cream that you just whip up. However, if you can't find coconut cream that's already been separated, this is how you extract the cream from a tin of full-fat coconut milk.

METHOD

Select a good-quality brand of full-fat coconut milk.

Chill the tin overnight in the refrigerator to harden (chilling in the freezer doesn't work as well). You want to separate the solidified cream at the top of the tin from the liquid. Chilling overnight is key, or the coconut cream won't harden and will probably be too soft to whip.

Before you whip the cream, chill a large mixing bowl in the freezer for 10 minutes.

Scoop the hardened cream into the bowl, leaving any clear liquid behind (reserve this for smoothies, soups and stews). Whip the cream with a handheld mixer or stand mixer until light peaks form. Be careful not to overmix.

Use the whipped cream immediately or, preferably, make ahead and chill for at least 4 hours after, which it will have firmed up even more!

COOK'S TIP:

If the coconut cream is too stiff when whipping, add some of the reserved liquid from the tin to help it whip more easily.

INDEX

*'There is no such thing as a
self made man/woman. We are
made up of thousands of others.
Everyone who has ever done a kind
deed for us, or spoken one word of
encouragement to us, has entered
into the makeup of our character
and of our thoughts, as well as our
success.'*

ACKNOWLEDGEMENTS

I usually don't write big thank yous because I always feel
that I might forget someone as there is so much and so many
to be thankful for. However this last year has shown that
support, friendships, family, love, community mean everything.

First of all I'd like to say thank you to my family. My parents
for their support and countless adventures around the world
and igniting my passion for food from a very young age.
My motherñ for always working hard and instilled that in me.
Roberto for being my biggest supporter and my love. We have
been through it all and come back stronger than ever.
P.S Thank you for listening to countless hours of meeping.
To Ayla for being the love of my life and my biggest fan,
everything I do is for you.

To Roberto's Big family – too many to count – that have
become my extended family.

To my little team, Nicole – Thank you for all that you do
and for getting us to the finishing line with this one! Is there
anything you can't do? Martine – for being a powerhouse
of a woman, for your support, kindness and for having my
back and being part of making this book happen. To Crab
Communications (Tess, Jess, Tom and Katherine) For taking
me on during the craziest of times, I feel like we are on
this journey together. Nick - for turning these recipes into
movable snippets so that they can be shared with everyone
and for always being a great food tester!

To my friends – you know who you are – I have a few but they
are the good kind.

Kate Pollard your friendship and guidance means the world.
Your uncanny support is undeniable and appreciated.

Thank you Hardie Grant for believing in me again. Kajal,
Eve, the Laura's, Ruth and more – for making this experience
so inclusive and creative.

To the incredible team of women who turned my recipes into
stunning images and made them all come to life. Lousie,
Sophie, Rachel what a dreamy week we had. Also to Nicole
and Niki who held the fort in the kitchen. Thank you to Gaya
Ceramics for some of the amazing ceramics on the shelves
behind me and in the book and my favourite coffee cup.

Shout out to my neighbours (you know who you are) for trying
endless deliveries of my dishes over lockdown and being my
testers when no one else could.

Most of all thank you to you reading this, for supporting what
I do, for cooking my recipes, for letting me do what I love
on a daily basis. It means an awful lot and for that I am so
grateful. Much Love.

Published in 2021 by Hardie Grant Books,
an imprint of Hardie Grant Publishing

Hardie Grant Books (London)
5th & 6th Floors
52–54 Southwark Street
London SE1 1UN

Hardie Grant Books (Melbourne)
Building 1, 658 Church Street
Richmond, Victoria 3121

hardiegrantbooks.com

All rights reserved. No part of this
publication may be reproduced, stored
in a retrieval system or transmitted
in any form by any means, electronic,
mechanical, photocopying, recording
or otherwise, without the prior written
permission of the publishers and
copyright holders.

The moral rights of the author
have been asserted.

Copyright text
© Bettina Campolucci-Bordi 2021

Copyright Photography
© Louise Hagger 2021

British Library Cataloguing-in-
Publication Data. A catalogue
record for this book is available
from the British Library.

Celebrate: Plant Based Recipes
for Every Occasion by
Bettina Campolucci-Bordi

ISBN: 978-1-78488-386-7

Publisher: Kajal Mistry
Commissioning Editor: Kate Pollard
Editor: Eve Marleau
Design: Claire Warner Studio
Photography: Louise Hagger
Copy Editor: Caroline West
Proofreader: Kate Wanwimolruk
Indexer: Vanessa Bird

Colour Reproduction by p2d
Printed and bound in China
by Leo Paper Products Ltd.

FSC
www.fsc.org

MIX
Paper from
responsible sources
FSC™ C020056